BRITISH SPORTS : PAST AND PRESENT

LAWN TENNIS

1 His late Majesty King George VI, as Duke of York, playing in the
Wimbledon Championships of 1926

BRITISH SPORTS : PAST & PRESENT

A Series Dedicated by Permission to
H.R.H. THE DUKE OF EDINBURGH

General Editor: Howard Marshall

LAWN TENNIS

By

Brigadier J. G. SMYTH
V.C. M.C. M.P.

LONDON
B. T. BATSFORD LTD

First Published, 1953

PRINTED AND BOUND IN GREAT BRITAIN BY JARROLD AND SONS LTD
LONDON AND NORWICH FOR THE PUBLISHERS
B. T. BATSFORD LTD
4 FITZHARDINGE STREET, PORTMAN SQUARE, LONDON W.1

FOREWORD

by

Group-Captain Sir Louis Greig, K.B.E., C.V.O., D.L.
(*Chairman of the All-England Club and the Wimbledon
Championships*)

I WAS both delighted and honoured when I was asked by
my friend Brigadier J. G. Smyth, V.C., M.C., M.P., to
write the Foreword to his story of the great game of
lawn tennis.

Jackie Smyth is indeed a fitting person to write a book on
this universally popular sport.

He has, of course, been a soldier—and very much a fighting
one—having fought with distinction and great gallantry in
both World Wars, and taken part in several other campaigns,
besides serving in various outposts of the Commonwealth.

In spite of his busy soldier's life, however, he found time to
become an all-round sportsman himself, representing the
Army in many sporting battles, not the least of which were
those of lawn tennis. He is a particularly enthusiastic
follower of boxing and, I must mention, no mean performer
on a horse, having been a Master of Foxhounds, a keen point-
to-point rider, pigsticker and polo player. Therefore, from
his own wide experience, this soldier sportsman writes with
authority and knowledge.

Owing to having become a Minister of the Crown he unfortunately has had to give up writing on lawn tennis for the
Sunday Times; but his articles on the game which, since the
war, have appeared every day in the Championships programme during the Wimbledon fortnight, have been a
familiar and looked-for pleasure by the countless Wimbledon
enthusiasts who come each year from all quarters of the
globe.

All followers of this splendid sport, in whichever country

they may live, will greet with pleasure, as I do, a history of lawn tennis, written by a man so well qualified to write it.

Brigadier Smyth tells us a fascinating tale of this fine game and its famous exponents; those men and women who with their sportsmanship and skill have woven for us the tapestry of lawn tennis through the years, from its small beginnings in the 1870's at the All-England Club, up to the present-day Championships with their absorbing excitement and world-wide appeal.

It is the story of a great game, and it is also the story of "Wimbledon".

LOUIS GREIG

All England Club, Wimbledon
26 January 1953

PREFACE

I HAVE been asked in this book to combine a concise history of the game from its early beginnings up to the present day with my own views on such controversial matters as the greatest players of each generation and of all time, and the professional "play-for-pay" game. As I have explained in the book it is a difficult business in any sport to compare champions of different generations, and I have no doubt that I shall at least have succeeded in making this part of the book controversial!

My thanks are due first to Sir Louis Greig, the distinguished and popular Chairman of the All-England Club and of the Wimbledon Championship Committee, who has kindly written a foreword to the book. Sir Louis partnered his late Majesty King George VI, when, as Duke of York, he competed in the Wimbledon doubles in 1926. And secondly to Colonel Duncan Macaulay, the well-known Secretary of the All-England Club, who has kindly read the script for me.

Lastly I would like to thank all those lawn tennis players and officials all over the world who have given me in such full measure their friendship and their hospitality.

Dolphin Square, London, S.W.1   J. G. SMYTH
January 1953

POSTSCRIPT

Since I wrote the above my friend Sir Louis Greig has passed on. When he knew he was dying he took the very greatest interest in this book as he felt it would be in some way a memory of those happy days at Wimbledon, watching the game he loved so much. Ill as he was, he took the greatest trouble over the Foreword, and I am sure it would be his wish that it should remain as a part of the book.

Dolphin Square, London, S.W.1   J. G. S.
March 1953

ACKNOWLEDGMENT

THE Author and Publishers wish to thank the following for their permission to reproduce the illustrations in this book:
Central Press Photos Ltd., for figs. 1, 17, 23, 28, 31, 48 and 49; L. H. J. Dorey, M.B.E. and *Lawn Tennis and Badminton*, for figs. 6 and 9; Fox Photos Ltd., for fig. 47; Keystone Press Agency Ltd., for figs. 16, 24, 34, 35, 41–3, 52 and 53; Mirrorpic, for figs. 20, 22, 25 and 33; New York Times Photos, for fig. 50; Picture Post Library, for figs. 2–5, 8 and 11; Sport & General Press Agency Ltd., for fig. 18; Topical Press Agency Ltd., for figs. 10, 15, 19, 21, 26, 27, 29, 30, 32, 36–40, 44, 45 and 50; United States Information Service, for fig. 54; Wide World Photos, for fig. 46.

Figs. 7 and 12 are reproduced from *Fifty Years of Wimbledon* by A. Wallis Myers, C.B.E. by permission of the All-England Lawn Tennis & Croquet Club.

The jacket, from a lithograph in the Library of Congress, Washington, is reproduced from material kindly supplied by the Bettmann Archive, New York.

CONTENTS

LIST OF ILLUSTRATIONS

Chapter One

THE EVOLUTION
OF THE GAME

LAWN TENNIS IS A young game—by comparison with such games as cricket—yet in the eighty years or so of its existence it has become possibly the most universally played game in the world. Every year some thirty or more of the lawn tennis nations enter teams to compete for the coveted Davis Cup, and every year more nations hold their own national championships for which, thanks to the ubiquitous aeroplane, the leading players of the world can compete. With a tennis racket in his kit the keen lawn tennis player, whether he be a "rabbit" or a star performer, can wander the world and there are few countries where he cannot find a court and an opponent worthy of his steel. Although championship lawn tennis, as it is played today, is as strenuous a sport as any which exists, and is very much a game for the highly trained young athlete, it can also be played—in a different tempo of course—with the keenest enjoyment by enthusiasts in their sixties and seventies. Such is the enthusiasm for the game today that Wimbledon will nowhere near hold the eager crowds of spectators who wish to come from all over the world to see the championships. Months before they take place, and long before the names of those competing are known, every bookable seat is sold, and thousands of pounds are returned each year to those who have been unlucky in the ballot. In the early days of the game's history lawn tennis was generally regarded as a summer pastime. Now the sun never sets on a lawn tennis championship meeting in some corner of the globe. Thanks to the International Lawn Tennis Federation, founded in

1915, the rules and general conduct of the game are co-ordinated and regulated the world over.

No one person can fairly claim to have "invented" the game of lawn tennis. It was really a break-away from the two older games of real tennis and rackets, and was popularised by a little band of enthusiasts at the All-England Croquet Club at Worple Road, Wimbledon, who wanted an out-door game of a more exciting and more mobile variety than croquet. But perhaps Major Walter Clopton Wingfield can best claim to have been the originator of lawn tennis when, in the early eighteen-seventies, he lodged his patent for the game which he called sphairistike, and the first game of the new lawn tennis was played on a grass court in Wales in 1873. However, it is only fair to say that a somewhat similar game had been played at Edgbaston by Mr. J. B. Pereira and Major T. H. Gem in 1868. Be that as it may, the game, as patented by Major Wingfield, became an immediate success. His balls and net were sold in Britain and abroad, and in 1874 officers of the British garrison in Bermuda were playing Major Wingfield's game and using his equipment and rules. Interest in the game soon began to widen, though it did so very gradually, and amongst a limited circle, mostly of somewhat elderly people. Then in 1875 a Code of Rules was published by the Marylebone Cricket Club and the new game was adopted by the All-England Croquet Club. So enthusiastic did the members become over the new game that in 1877 the name of the Club was changed to "The All-England Croquet and Lawn Tennis Club", and in 1877 the first Lawn Tennis Championships were played at the old Wimbledon at Worple Road. Shortly afterwards the Marylebone Cricket Club renounced its authority over the game in favour of the All-England Club.

Unlike almost every other game lawn tennis from its earliest days centred round a place and a name—Wimbledon. It found a headquarters in the All-England Club, and from that central core lawn tennis spread all over the world. Today the British Lawn Tennis Association has over 3,000 affiliated clubs and schools.

In the year 1874 an American lady, Miss Outerbridge, obtained equipment for Wingfield's game from the British

2 A group of early English champions of the late nineteenth century. Note the styles of dress and the popular square-headed racket. *From left to right:* E. de S. H. Browne; E. Renshaw; Rev. J. T. Hartley; Miss Watson; C. W. Grinstead; Miss Maud Watson; H. F. Lawford; W. Renshaw

3   The famous Doherty brothers, **R. F.** (*left*) and **H. L.** (*right*), who between 1897 and 1906 dominated the lawn tennis scene

Officers' Mess in Bermuda and took it to the United States, where lawn tennis was first played in that country at Camp Washington. The United States Lawn Tennis Association, the oldest Lawn Tennis Association, was founded in 1881 when the first U.S.A. Championships were held. At these championships the English rules were adopted and an English ball, made by Ayres, was used. There are now over 1,115 clubs in the United States, and it is estimated that there are some 12,000 lawn tennis courts.

In 1875 the new game spread to Brazil and India. In Brazil lawn tennis was first played at the Rio de Janeiro Cricket Club, while the first tournament in that country was played in 1911 at the Fluminese Football Club. Brazil is now rapidly becoming a lawn tennis nation to be reckoned with.

Lawn tennis was introduced into India by British residents in 1875, and ten years later the first tournament was played at Lahore under the title of the "Punjab Lawn Tennis Championships". In 1949 India staged the first "Championships of Asia", which were played at the famous Calcutta South Club in December of that year. India and Pakistan, which together made up the old India, have sent many fine players to Wimbledon, both British and Indian.

In 1876 lawn tennis reached the Continent of Europe and was first played at Bad Homburg in Germany by two British visitors. By 1883 Hamburg had three courts, and very soon afterwards lawn tennis was played in nearly all the big cities in Germany. The first championships were held at Hamburg in 1887. Today in Western Germany there are more than 800 clubs, and over 100 tournaments are held annually—despite the setback of the war. Although a German male has never yet managed to win a Wimbledon championship Germany had the runner-up in the men's singles in 1914 in O. Froitzheim, and that fine player Gottfried von Cramm was runner-up to Britain's F. J. Perry in 1935 and 1936 and to America's Donald Budge in 1937. Germany did, however, have the distinction of providing one female Wimbledon champion in the shape of Fräulein Cilly Aussem, who won the Wimbledon singles in 1931.

In 1877 lawn tennis established itself in the holiday resorts of France and is now one of the leading games of the country.

France has a wonderful record in International play, and in the days of the incomparable Suzanne Lenglen and of the famous "Four Musketeers", Lacoste, Borotra, Cochet and Brugnon, France ruled the world of lawn tennis.

In 1878 lawn tennis was first played in Australia when an asphalt court was laid at the Melbourne Cricket Club. The first tournament in Australia, the Victoria Championships, was played at the Melbourne Cricket Club in 1880. Since those days Australia has been constantly amongst the premier lawn tennis nations of the world.

Before the end of the nineteenth century Sweden, Italy, Hungary, Peru, Denmark, Switzerland, Argentina, the Netherlands, Jamaica, Greece, Turkey, the Lebanon, Egypt, Finland, South Africa and Colombia had adopted the new game.

When lawn tennis began it was a game for the leisured classes. It was introduced when the craze for croquet had begun to pall and golf had hardly got going. It started as a garden party game for the upper classes. There were no public courts and few open competitions except at the centres of the game, and it was not until after the World War of 1914–18 that it started to spread throughout the community. It was then that the National Press began to devote their space to it; professional coaches came into existence and the game spread like wildfire.

The original rules of the game drawn up by the Tennis Committee of the M.C.C. in 1875 were by no means perfect. They adopted at first the hour-glass shaped court invented by Major Wingfield. The scoring was by "hand-in" and "hand-out" as in rackets, and "hand-in" alone could serve and score. The balls were $2\frac{1}{4}$ inches in diameter and $1\frac{1}{2}$ oz. in weight. By the time, however, that the first Wimbledon Championships were held in 1877 the rules had been altered considerably. The court was made rectangular, 26 yards long by 9 yards wide, the net being fixed to posts 3 feet outside the court. Tennis scoring was adopted entirely, and in the service one fault was allowed without penalty. It is a remarkable tribute to the 1877 Wimbledon committee that these rules have stood the test of time and are still law.

Some of the other earlier rules have, of course, undergone

changes—particularly with regard to the height of the net and the size and weight of the balls. By the 1877 rules the height of the net was 5 feet at the posts and 3 feet 3 inches at the centre. The first champion, Mr. Spencer W. Gore, an old Harrovian and a racket player, took full advantage of this fact to launch an intensive net attack, knowing that he could not easily be passed down the side-lines. The balls used at the first championships had to be made specially for the occasion and were hand-sewn into white cloth covers. There was, of course, no regulation as to the bounce or hardness of the balls, and the difficulties of the early champions were vastly increased by reason of the fact that no two balls were anywhere near the same in performance. It was not until the nineteen-twenties that bounce and hardness tests were insti-tuted—and these have, of course, been tightened up and improved with the passage of time.

At the original Wimbledon "sudden death" was called after "five-all", and players changed courts after every set, instead of, as they do now, after the first, third, and then every odd game. We learn that there were twenty-two com-petitors at the first Wimbledon; that the tournament was adjourned over the Eton and Harrow match, and about 200 spectators watched the final, paying one shilling entrance. The overhead service was, of course, unknown in those early days; the server either served a shoulder-high delivery or an underhand ball with plenty of cut.

The early rackets were curious pear-shaped affairs—far heavier than those in use at the present day. They were adopted from the game of real tennis. The best rackets, the frames of which were of rent ash, were well seasoned and really did last for ever. The highest quality racket cost as much as forty shillings, which was considered a colossal price in those days, but only about half what a good racket costs today. The gut was much coarser than that used in modern rackets and much less tightly strung, which was, of course, the reason it lasted so long. Nevertheless many of the early players managed to make the ball travel remarkably fast. It was many years before the oval-headed racket came into use. Up to the early 'nineties most of the best rackets had a slightly flattened top and some of the leading Australian players retained this old-fashioned shape until the nineteen-thirties.

Many people do not realise that it is efficiency only which governs the implement used for hitting the ball and that, even today, there is no rule which limits the size, weight or method of manufacture of a lawn tennis racket.

By the 1880 Wimbledon Championships considerable advances had been made in the game's administration. A lease of the ground for another twelve years was obtained and some extra stands and dressing-room accommodation constructed. The hand-stitched ball disappeared in favour of the Ayres ball. Twelve courts were now in use and the Wimbledon entry increased to sixty, the charge for admission being raised from one shilling to half a crown. The net was lowered at the posts from 5 feet to 4 feet; the service line was brought in to a distance of 21 feet from the net; the size and weight of the balls were fixed; certain alterations were made regarding the position of the feet for service and a service ball touching the net was ruled to be a let; and a player was forbidden to touch the net or to volley the ball until it had passed the net. With the exception that the net has since been lowered another 6 inches at the posts—to 3 feet 6 inches, that the server must now have both feet behind the baseline, and that the players change ends after every odd game, the 1880 rules have in principle lasted to the present day.

In 1882 the word "Croquet" was expunged from the nomenclature of the All-England Club, and it was not until twenty years later that it was again included—for sentimental and historical reasons—but this time "Croquet" appeared after "Lawn Tennis" instead of before. The Club then became known as it is today as "The All-England Lawn Tennis and Croquet Club".

The year 1883 was noteworthy at Wimbledon for the visit of C. M. and J. S. Clark, the pioneers of the American lawn tennis invasion; and in 1884 a Ladies' Championship was instituted which was won by Miss Maud Watson from an entry of thirteen.

Although the game of lawn tennis was obviously gaining in popularity the number of entries at Wimbledon continued to be very low. In 1885 there were only twenty-three entries, though no less than 3,500 spectators watched the challenge round. In 1886 both the men's doubles and ladies' singles were given challenge rounds which meant that the holders did not have to play their way through the events as they do now. In 1901 the Slazengers ball was used at Wimbledon for the first time, and Messrs. Slazengers still supply the balls used at Wimbledon today.

The reign of the Dohertys, which opened in 1897 and continued virtually for ten years, not only revived interest in the Wimbledon Championships, but stimulated the spread of the game all over the world. By the beginning of the new century crowds were flocking to Wimbledon.

The Dohertys retired in 1906 and in the next year, for the first time, all three championships were won by overseas players. From then until the outbreak of the First World War the American challenge became ever stronger, but thanks to that great Australasian pair of Brookes and Wilding and to the gallant English veteran, A. W. Gore, the Wimbledon singles championship never went outside the Empire, although M. Decugis and A. H. Gobert of France succeeded in lifting the doubles championship in 1911.

During the four years of the First World War competitive sport in Europe closed down completely, whereas in America the interregnum was much shorter. When a war-weary world turned back with a sigh of relief to sport, America's lawn tennis players were at once supreme. This was a natural and quite inevitable state of affairs and was assisted by the high degree of organisation which had developed the game in the United States and had extended it into their colleges and schools.

For over four years Wimbledon had been closed, as far as lawn tennis was concerned, and it had been a difficult job to keep the All-England Club going. A good many tournaments failed to revive at all after the war, and others took some time to get on their feet again. However, such great enthusiasm was shown on the part of the public that it was decided to recommence the Wimbledon Championships in 1919. The announcement was heralded by an unprecedented demand for seats and a very large entry of players. To cope with the former a ballot was necessary, and machinery was set up for the entries to be restricted by a selection sub-committee over which the new Wimbledon referee, Mr. F. R. Burrow, who had succeeded Mr. H. S. Scrivener, presided. In actual fact the committee did not have to exercise their powers as 129 entries were received for the men's singles of which one dropped out and 128 were accepted. This is the same number as are accepted at the new Wimbledon today.

The years following the First World War were great years for Wimbledon and for lawn tennis generally. The magnetic personalities and wonderful play of W. T. Tilden and Mlle Suzanne Lenglen drew enormous crowds to Wimbledon. Then came the reign of the famous "Four Musketeers" of France—Lacoste, Borotra, Cochet and Brugnon—followed by the British comeback led by F. J. Perry and H. W. Austin.

In 1922 the All-England Club changed its place of residence from Worple Road to Church Road, Wimbledon. For some time it had been evident that Worple Road could no longer provide adequate accommodation for the crowds who wanted to see the championships. In 1920 the purchase and equipment of the new Wimbledon in Church Road had been completed for a sum of approximately £140,000, after a working agreement had been reached between the All-England Club and the Lawn Tennis Association, the governing body of the game. The new Wimbledon was opened by the King, on June 26th, 1922. The imposing new Centre Court was able to accommodate 15,000 spectators, three times as many as its old counterpart in Worple Road. Number 1 Court, which was situated next door to it, had a capacity for nearly 5,000, and Numbers 2 and 3 Courts, though not covered, were equipped with special stands. It was inevitable that the new Wimbledon should lack some of the homely atmosphere of the old, but it soon assimilated its traditions whilst having much better facilities both for the players and the public.

It was most unfortunate that the opening of the new ground should have coincided with the wettest fortnight in the whole history of the championships, which took fifteen days to finish instead of the normal twelve. Nevertheless the entry was a record; there were many attendances by the Royal Family and thousands of would-be spectators had to be turned away. Despite the appalling weather the gates had to be closed on three days of the meeting.

Besides the change of ground, 1922 saw an important change in procedure. The challenge round was abolished in all three events: men's singles, ladies' singles and men's doubles. This change had long been advocated but, when it came to the point, tradition had always proved too strong. Mlle Lenglen, the only holder concerned, expressed her perfect willingness to play through and there was general approval for the innovation. It is impossible to estimate what the effect of the old procedure had been, but it is extremely doubtful whether a player such as R. F. Doherty, of fine strokes but frail physique and indifferent health, could ever have won the singles championship four years running had he been forced to play through the whole event. On the other hand, a player such as the New Zealander, A. F. Wilding, a magnificent physical specimen who throve on hard work and match competition, might well have retained his championship in 1914, had he been able to sharpen himself up by playing right through the event.

The 1924 Wimbledon saw a further break with tradition in the form of a modified seeding of the draw by which "nominated" players, not exceeding four from any one country, were separated as widely as possible from one another in the draw. This step, which had already been taken by most other countries, prevented two players from the same country, who had perhaps travelled half the world to get to Wimbledon, from playing one another in the first round. In 1924 twenty different nations were represented in the men's singles. And in this year Wimbledon gave up the title of "The Championships of the World" and became known as "The Championships". Nevertheless lawn tennis players the world over continued to regard Wimbledon as their "Mecca" and the winning of a championship there as their highest goal.

By this time so many more entries were received than could be accepted that in 1925 qualifying rounds were held at the Roehampton Club. Today Northern and Southern qualifying rounds have to be held, each becoming little championships in themselves.

The Wimbledon Championships celebrated their golden Jubilee in 1926, their fiftieth anniversary. The occasion was marked by collecting together all the surviving winners of the championships since their inception in 1877 for a presentation of commemorative medals by King George V and Queen Mary(18). There was a good attendance of champions led by P. F. Hadow, who won the men's singles in 1878, and Miss Maud Watson, winner of the ladies' singles in 1884 and 1885. There was tremendous enthusiasm as the King and Queen entered the Centre Court to the strains of the National Anthem, took up their position at the table and the long procession of champions began. As each stepped forward the secretary, Commander Hillyard, announced the name and championship year of the recipients. Jean Borotra of France made yet another of his dramatic entries, rushing on to the court just in time, having flown over from France at the last minute.

The 1926 Wimbledon was also marked by the entry of the Duke of York, afterwards King George VI, in the men's doubles, with his equerry, Sir Louis Greig, who is now chairman of the All-England Club(1). They were unlucky enough to meet two former champions in A. W. Gore and H. Roper Barrett, and were eliminated in the first round. The match was played on Number 2 Court and drew a great crowd. His Royal Highness thoroughly enjoyed his match, and, although he never competed at Wimbledon again, he maintained his interest in the game and in the championships.

The Jubilee year also marked a change of secretary for the All-England Club. Commander G. W. Hillyard, who had served as secretary from 1907 to 1925, was succeeded by Mr. Dudley Larcombe, husband of the former lady champion. Mr. Larcombe remained secretary until the outbreak of the Second World War—which he did not survive.

An important innovation was made at Wimbledon in 1927 in the seeding of the draw in all events. This procedure is not entirely popular with those who only have tickets for the first days of the championships as it prevents an early clash of the highest ranked players; but it does ensure that these players generally come through the earlier rounds and it has for many years been the custom in all the major championships.

The coming of World War II in 1939 put a stop to lawn tennis more completely than it did to most other forms of sport. Football of a sort can be played in most places and on most surfaces, but the lawn tennis court—particularly, of course, the grass variety—does require a certain amount of constant attention and must be of a certain standard for tournament play to be possible at all.

America continued her national championships throughout the war, but in Britain, with the exception of a few exhibition matches, lawn tennis closed down completely during the war years as it did, of course, on the continent of Europe. The All-England Club became a Civil Defence Centre and the Centre Court a place of ghosts. The National Fire Service occupied the space and the rooms round Number 2 Court. Then came the Army, first the Welsh Guards and then the London Irish. Later the Club became a Home Guard headquarters.

After the death of the secretary, Major D. R. Larcombe, Miss Nora Cleather, who had been assistant secretary for some years, took over the management of the Club, and did a magnificent job keeping the place going under most adverse and often frightening conditions. The Club was badly bombed, the Centre Court getting a direct hit and the whole place being strewn with debris. Some say this was an act of revenge on the part of a German pilot whose entry at Wimbledon had been refused! But Miss Cleather and her small staff worked overtime to keep the courts and equipment in shape against the happy day when Wimbledon would re-echo once more to the sound of tennis racket hitting ball, and to the cheers of the watching crowds—instead of to the eternal tramp of marching feet. On sunny days the huge tarpaulins were hauled out for an airing and the courts were weeded and looked after. Players from the Forces would often dash down to Wimbledon for a game, and were always made welcome.

But most other lawn tennis clubs in Britain suffered worse than Wimbledon. Many suffered material damage from bombing and some were completely destroyed. Others mouldered into decay through lack of staff attention. Not only was there a general mobilisation of all Britain's young men, but Britain called up her women too to a degree exceeding that of any other lawn tennis playing nation. And when the players were eventually released with the coming of peace there were no courts, clubs and professional coaches waiting for them. The established players never recovered from a tennis gap of five long years, and the next generation never got started.

Looking at the debris of war and the stark desolation of the scene at the All-England Club on the day peace was finally declared I found it difficult to imagine how the championships could ever be started again in 1946. However, just as British lawn tennis had grown up around Wimbledon originally, so the All-England Club, with its permanent partner, the Lawn Tennis Association, now gave the lead to a British and world lawn tennis revival.

At the end of the war Lieut.-Colonel A. D. C. Macaulay, one of the leading British lawn tennis referees, was appointed secretary to the All-England Club with Miss Bompas as his assistant. They continue to grow in efficiency and popularity with every year that passes. When the Wimbledon referee, Mr. F. R. Burrow, retired in 1936 after eighteen years in that office he was succeeded by Mr. Hamilton Price, who died during the war and was succeeded in his turn by Captain A. K. Trower. Captain Trower, who had been severely wounded in World War I, and most gallantly made light of his disabilities, himself died in harness in 1950 and was succeeded in 1951 by his assistant, Colonel W. J. Legg.

No one will ever realise how much work Colonel Macaulay and his little band of helpers had to put in before the first post-war Wimbledon was staged in 1946. There were grave shortages of labour, materials and equipment which made it impossible to repair the bomb damage on the Centre Court. This resulted in 1,000 seats being out of use.

But from the moment it was decided that the championships should be held their success was assured. It seemed as though the whole lawn tennis world wanted to make a pilgrimage to the Mecca of the game. Entries were received from thirty-two nations, and it was soon obvious that far more people would want to watch the play than the All-England Club could possibly hold.

It was only natural that the United States should face the post-war scene as the strongest lawn tennis playing nation in the world. Their young men had, of course, been called up for active service like the rest, but the clubs, the courts and the tournaments were kept going all through the war, with the result that the leading players were soon back into their stride. Women's tennis in America continued intensively throughout the war and when peace was declared the Americans sallied forth to conquer the world with their rackets. But it was not long before Australia returned to the attack in the men's events, and the post-war years have developed into a great struggle for the major prizes between Australia and the United States.

Has the game altered much in the first seventy-five years of Wimbledon Championships? Yes, of course it has, since its very early years, because those were years of trial and error as far as strokes and tactics were concerned. But since the Doherty era at the turn of the century the developments in play have not been very marked considering the improvements which have been made in rackets, balls and court surfaces. I doubt whether there have been any faster services and smashes than Gerald Patterson's in 1922; any fiercer forehand drives than W. M. Johnston's in 1923; any better backhand drives than Lacoste's or more devastating volleys than Borotra's; nor has anyone ever taken an earlier ball than Henri Cochet. For all that I do think that the men's game has become more aggressive and dynamic: the rallies have tended to become shorter and the advance to the net is made earlier.

In women's tennis we have seen an attempt made by Miss Alice Marble, Mrs. du Pont and Miss Louise Brough to take the femininity of stroke out of women's tennis. Certainly such serves and smashes have never been seen in women's tennis before. Nevertheless players with sound and accurate ground strokes such as Miss Pauline Betz, Miss Doris Hart and Miss Maureen Connolly have found a vulnerable gap in the women's "big game"—and punctured some nasty holes in it. I believe that the best game of Suzanne Lenglen and Helen Wills-Moody would still be good enough to beat the world today.

It is perhaps in the costumes of the players that there has been the greatest evolution. At the early Wimbledons knickerbockers and a striped football jersey was quite a favourite costume for men. But garden party and country-house tennis demanded a much more ornate appearance, and it was even rather bad form to appear in shirt-sleeves. Tennis "blazers" of every sort of shade were as fashionable for lawn tennis as they were for cricket, and the real experts at the game wore long white blanket coats off the courts, which were generally referred to as "owe-forty" coats. You really had to be very handsome or rather a good player to get away with these. By the turn of the century white shirts and white trousers had become the accepted wear for men for tournament tennis as well as for the garden party variety. This form of garb was worn to perfection by the famous Doherty brothers, both of whom preferred not to roll up the sleeves of their shirts. R. F. Doherty, "Big Do", generally wore his shirt sleeves flapping and H. L. Doherty, "Little Do", had his buttoned at the wrists. An elastic waist belt was generally worn by both of them. As the Dohertys both looked perfect on the court and played perfectly into the bargain, what was good enough for them was good enough for anybody—and people copied their appearance as well as their strokes. Both in men's and women's fashions on the court it has usually been very difficult for anyone to make a startling change unless it is adopted by one of the star performers. But even in the Doherty days rolled up shirt sleeves were quite permissible for most players. Gradually the waist belt gave place to some sort of side elastic or buckle fastening, and the loose tennis shirt gave way to the tighter fitting form of tennis vest.

Britain's Bunny Austin was one of the pioneers of shorts, and when he first wore them at Wimbledon they came in for a good deal of adverse criticism. However, as the innovation was obviously sensible for one of the most strenuous sports, in the world—and Austin was one of the leading performers —others started to copy his appearance as they started to copy his strokes. By the time the post-war Wimbledons had started shorts were becoming more and more popular. Nevertheless up to 1947 no one had won the Wimbledon singles in shorts. When Kramer did so that year the death knell of "longs" had been sounded and they are now almost a curiosity. F. R. Schroeder (U.S.A.) the Wimbledon singles champion of 1949, epitomised the last word in men's tennis attire, a thin short-sleeved gym vest, attenuated running shorts, socks and gym shoes. At Forest Hills that year he wore spiked shoes and looked even more what he was—a runner on the tennis courts. The wheel of men's lawn tennis attire has turned full circle; the knickerbockers and vests of the eighteen-seventies, the football clothes of that day, were the rig for men at Wimbledon when the game started. The football kit of today, a vest and shorts, is now the almost universal wear for championship lawn tennis—and a very sensible one too. If the vests and shorts are well cut and well fitting, what could look nicer? They are shown off to perfection by South Africa's Eric Sturgess, Britain's Tony Mottram and Australia's Frank Sedgman. It looks as though this fashion has become permanent and indeed the only thing the men could cast off is their shirts—but I doubt if we shall live to see that at Wimbledon. Even the pocket handkerchief is now discarded and the very un-Doherty-like habit has arisen of wiping the heated brow on the shoulder during play, with a thorough bath-towelling when necessary at the referee's chair on changing ends. Manufacturers, in despair at having nothing further to invent for men, have managed to popularise white woollen wristlets to keep the hands dry. As spiked shoes are never allowed on the sacred turf of Wimbledon some players have started to appear in ridged or knobbed shoes which tear great chunks out of the courts and will certainly incur the displeasure of the management—if not of the other players.

Women's tennis dress remained stubbornly conventional—and one would have thought thoroughly unsuitable—for quite a long time; but, of course, women did not play at Wimbledon until seven years after the men had played their first championship. Straw hats, close fitting blouses, voluminous skirts reaching almost to the ground were the order of the day for the early champions. Yet the fact remains that they played extremely well and were amazingly mobile in clothes which our modern tennis girls would think were quite impossible. Just as men's tennis fashions tended to follow those of the champion of the day so, for the same reasons, women's tennis fashions showed little change up to the end of the First World War. At that time Mrs. Lambert Chambers had won the pre-war ladies' singles no less than seven times and was generally regarded as being the greatest woman player in the world. When she returned to the courts in 1919 to defend her title the only concession she had made to the passing of time since her first victory at Wimbledon in 1903 was that her long sleeved blouse was open at the neck and her skirt was a little shorter. Her opponent in the challenge round was Mlle Suzanne Lenglen, then twenty years of age, and playing at Wimbledon for the first time. Had Mrs. Lambert Chambers won this tremendous match who knows what would have happened to women's lawn tennis fashions? But the coming of Suzanne Lenglen marked not an evolution in women's attire but a revolution. She discarded long sleeves, suspender belt and petticoats at one fell swoop and sped about the court in a pleated skirt and stockings held up by garters above the knee, showing large expanses of bare leg whenever she jumped for a smash or stretched for a volley. It took a very great champion to get away with that, and the world of Wimbledon was shocked to the core. But Suzanne was a very great champion and everyone had to acknowledge that her eccentricities of dress were all conducive to freer movement on the court. Where she showed the way the whole feminine lawn tennis world followed. They not only copied her strokes but they copied her bandeaux and her costumes.

But it was not until 1929, three years after the passing of Lenglen from the Wimbledon scene, that a South African girl, Miss Tapscott, greatly daring, appeared at Wimbledon without stockings. What a stir that caused! Would the committee forbid her to appear on court? Wisely the authorities maintained a discreet silence. There should be a small statue of Miss Tapscott in the All-England Club, for she certainly rendered a great service to women's tennis. Within a few years bare legs for women tennis players became universal. And soon men players had started to display their nether limbs to the public gaze.

In 1934 the American women's Wightman Cup team

appeared at Wimbledon in shorts, and thenceforward shorts or short skirts became the recognised wear for women players. Miss Alice Marble of the United States and Miss Kay Stammers (afterwards Mrs. Menzies) of Great Britain, the finalists at the 1939 Wimbledon, symbolised the last word in tennis dress, combining the maximum utility with the height of attractiveness in two particularly attractive wearers. Alice Marble adopted the more boyish costume of brief rather close-fitting shorts, whilst Kay Stammers wore fuller shorts or a short skirt.

There have been no further developments since then from a utility standpoint. Indeed it is difficult to see how there well could be, although various attempts have been made to add charm by the addition of frills and coloured ribbons. But these have generally died a natural death because, firstly, they don't add to the mobility and freedom of the wearer and generally have the quite fatal effect of making her self-conscious on court; and, secondly, because up to the present the rather *outré* fashions have wisely been eschewed by the champions. And if in the future some tennis designer should manage to persuade a lady champion to make of herself a mannequin on court there will come some "blue flash" like Marjorie Jackson, the famous Australian Olympic sprinter, clad in simple vest and shorts who will cut out the frills and get on with the game—and then the fashions will change again. But the real champions can look attractive on court in the simplest costumes, and it is always a case of "handsome is as handsome does". No one could look nicer on court than the great women champions of the post-war tennis world such as Louise Brough and Doris Hart in their simple, beautifully cut tennis dresses—and how well they play in them!

As I have said earlier on in this chapter the rules of lawn tennis have altered very little since the quite early days of Wimbledon—and indeed there has been little demand for change. Every now and then when some devastating server appears people start to clamour for there to be only one service ball instead of two; just as some people demand that the wicket should be widened when a Don Bradman appears on the cricket scene. But always, in the tennis world, some counter has appeared such as Henri Cochet who took Tilden's cannon balls on the rise and turned their speed to his own advantage. There is, however, one rule which causes never ending controversy and dissatisfaction—and that is the foot-fault rule. There are more international incidents, bad feeling and crowd disturbances over this rule, both in Davis Cup matches and national championships, than over any other matter. In brief the rule says that the server shall throughout the delivery of the service:

(*a*) Not change his position by walking or running;
(*b*) Maintain contact with the ground;
(*c*) Keep both feet behind the baseline.

From the umpire's chair (*a*) can be checked easily; but it is the combination of (*b*) and (*c*) which is so difficult to determine, even by an experienced foot-fault judge. Most modern servers—particularly when they are going to follow their services to the net—finish their service on the toes of their left foot and with their right foot in the air. It is comparatively easy, even from the umpire's chair, to check whether or not the left foot has maintained contact with the ground—provided one watches the left foot. But one man cannot watch the left foot for jump, the right foot for swing, and at the same time look at the ball so that he can be certain that it has not been struck before the right foot swings over the line.

In small tournaments they just cannot cope with it at all and the players get into bad foot-fault habits. In the big championships one foot-fault judge may constantly penalise one player whose service another expert may consider to be all right. Neither the crowd nor the player himself knows whether he is being penalised for jump or swing, or both—unless he stops play to ask—and then he is generally acutely dissatisfied with the answer.

The Umpires' Association in Great Britain, the Lawn Tennis Association of the United States and the International Lawn Tennis Federation have all been concerned about this matter for some time—and well they may be.

There is one rule of international lawn tennis which is not observed in the Wimbledon Championships, and that is the ten minutes rest in men's matches after the third set and in women's after the second. At Wimbledon play is continuous throughout a match. The ten minutes rest does sometimes decide the result of a match, and there are often complaints from exhausted losers about the Wimbledon procedure. On the other hand, the ten minutes is apt to be abused and is often much nearer twenty.

So much then for a brief review of the evolution of the game before I start to examine in more detail the play and the players. The chief events of the modern lawn tennis year are the Davis Cup and the four major national championships—France, Wimbledon, America and Australia. The Americans divide their nationals into two parts, playing the doubles first at Boston and the singles and mixed doubles at Forest Hills. But of these four the greatest of all remains "the Championships" at Wimbledon. I have never met a world ranking player, male or female, who has not regarded the courts, the organisation, the hospitality and the quality of the play at Wimbledon as being second to none in the world.

I cannot close this chapter, however, without making some reference to the International Lawn Tennis Club which was founded by A. Wallis Myers in 1924. The inspiration for starting the Club was born from a casual conversation between Lord Balfour and Wallis Myers during the Wimbledon Championships of 1923. Doubtless the sight of so many nations engaged in friendly rivalry gave Lord Balfour the idea of forming some concrete society among them. Something that would not only emphasise the sporting spirit in which the game is played and the friendship created among the players of all nations, but would consolidate and encourage that spirit and those friendships in a living body. Lord Balfour's inspiration, combined with the organising genius of Wallis Myers, gave birth to this brotherhood of players which has grown to dimensions which must be far beyond the dreams of those pioneers.

The first International Club was that of Great Britain, to which the I.C.'s of France, U.S.A., the Netherlands, Sweden, Belgium, Argentina, Denmark, South Africa, India and Australia have since become affiliated. The ideals of sportsmanship for which the I.C. stands have had a definite influence for good on the modern development of the game. They cannot be summarised better than in those words of Sir Henry Newbolt which the Club have taken as their motto:

> To set the Cause above renown,
> To love the game beyond the prize,
> To honour, while you strike him down,
> The foe that comes with fearless eyes,
> To count the life of battle good,
> And dear the land that gave you birth;
> And dearer yet the brotherhood
> That binds the brave of all the earth.

Chapter Two

THE YEARS BEFORE
THE FIRST WORLD WAR

ALTHOUGH THE NEW lawn tennis plant had soon found
firm roots in what was to be its spiritual home, the
All-England Club at Worple Road, Wimbledon, it was
for some time a somewhat fragile growth. It had no prece-
dents and no traditions and might well have faded into
obscurity or become a mere garden party social diversion
had not two athletes of strong personality revealed its
potentialities as a vigorous competitive sport. The Renshaw
twins were undoubtedly the real fathers of modern lawn
tennis(12). They had been educated at Cheltenham and they
made their début at Wimbledon in 1880 when they were
nineteen. Although they were neither of them successful at
their first attempt they dominated the game practically all
through the eighties. Willie Renshaw was a slightly stronger
player than his brother, Ernest, and he held the championship six years running, from 1881 to 1886, and won it once again
in 1889. The curious thing was that, although Ernest only
won the championship once, most of the best players of the
day would rather have played Willie than Ernest. But the
fact remains that in constant practice against one another on
a fast and true tar asphalt surface they laid the foundations
of the strokes and tactics of the game as we know it today.

In 1887 the women's championship at Wimbledon was won
by Miss Lottie Dod(7), who had previously won the Irish
title, at the age of fifteen. Between that year and 1893 she
won the championship five times; she then retired from the
lawn tennis arena and took up golf and won the championship. She was also a hockey international and the best

woman archer in the country. Although it is difficult to compare Miss Dod with the moderns, because she did not have anything like the opposition—when she won her first title there were only five competitors in the ladies' singles—she was a remarkable player. She played the all-court game in advance of her time, volleyed with great strength and accuracy and had a powerful smash. This was all the more remarkable in that she served underhand. And what a lot of women who came after her would have benefited by adopting a good cut underhand service instead of fatiguing themselves with serving overhand a service which, in so many cases, merely sat up and asked to be slaughtered! But the chief characteristic of Miss Dod's game was its effortless ease. Her anticipation was so good that she never seemed to be hurried.

As the nineteenth century entered upon its last ten years lawn tennis fell rather into the doldrums. The public were reacting from the Renshaw boom and no other personalities had arisen to take their place. Then suddenly, out of a rather grey sky, appeared the two brightest stars which have ever graced the British lawn tennis firmament. The Doherty era started in 1897 when Reggie, "Big Do", beat the holder, H. S. Mahoney in the challenge round. For the next ten years one or other of the two brothers won the singles nine times; and in partnership they won the doubles eight times (3). It is curious to note that in the first thirty years of Wimbledon three pairs of brothers (two of them twins) carried off the singles championship no fewer than twenty times and the doubles nineteen times. The Dohertys have had few equals before or since as singles players, and as a doubles pair they were certainly one of the very best of all. Their perfect court manners, attractive personalities and appearance, together with the super-excellence of their style and play, drew enormous crowds wherever they took the courts. Reggie was two years older than Laurie, "Little Do", but they were both at Westminster together and then went on to Cambridge University.

Those who knew the two brothers well differed as to which was the finer player. Laurie certainly had the better playing record because his brother's health was never very good—even in his best match playing days. Indeed it is doubtful whether "R.F." could have won the Wimbledon singles four years running if he had had to play through the whole event as the modern champions have to do. Laurie was far quicker about the court and much more severe on the volley and overhead, but "R.F." 's wonderful topspin backhand drive, extreme accuracy and uncanny anticipation were phenomenal. They disliked playing against one another and seldom did so if they could possibly avoid it. Both the Dohertys died tragically young in their thirties.

The effect of the Dohertys on the drooping fortunes of Wimbledon, and on lawn tennis generally, was quite incalculable. Wimbledon profits started to boom and the triumphs of the brothers on the Continent and in America lit a torch of enthusiasm for the game all over the world. At Wimbledon the two brothers experienced challenging opposition in the singles, particularly from A. W. Gore(5), who was gradually developing the severe and accurate baseline game which was subsequently to make him Wimbledon champion three times, and from the west countryman, S. H. Smith, of the terrific forehand drive. But the latter, formidable as he was—and particularly to overseas players—never succeeded in beating either of the Dohertys at Wimbledon.

In 1898 H. L. Doherty did challenge his brother for the singles title, but had the very greatest difficulty in defeating the previous holder, H. S. Mahoney. In the challenge round "R.F." lost two sets to his brother in a somewhat colourless and uninspiring match. Neither of the brothers ever seemed to have any stomach for the fight when they were opposed to one another. In this they were quite different from their predecessors, the Renshaws, who delighted in having a crack at one another.

In 1899 the Wimbledon field continued to be domestic. H. L. Doherty was not well enough to enter for the singles, the final of which was contested between A. W. Gore and S. H. Smith after that clever player, H. Roper Barrett, had very nearly beaten Smith in a terrific five-set match of sixty-four games. Gore beat Smith in the final and actually took the first two sets off "R.F." in the challenge round and then was very decisively beaten. The Dohertys gained their second consecutive doubles victory.

Nineteen hundred saw the fourth successive victory of R. F. Doherty at Wimbledon. S. H. Smith beat Gore, who had defeated "H.L.", and "R.F." duly defeated Smith in the challenge round. For the fourth year running the Dohertys won the doubles.

The general tempo of the game had quickened at the turn of the century and America began to come very definitely into the Wimbledon picture. In 1901 Dwight Davis and Holcombe Ward, the American doubles champions, were a pair very much to be reckoned with. With their black shoes and their sinister "American" twist services, at that time unknown in England, they seemed almost to mesmerise the home players. But in the challenge round the Doherty brothers only took one set to acclimatise themselves to this novel form of attack and then won fairly comfortably for the fifth successive year. Nineteen hundred and one, however, witnessed the end of R. F. Doherty's reign as singles champion. "H.L." was beaten by G. W. Hillyard, who had the very worst of bad luck in losing to Gore by a net-cord stroke when he was within a point of the match. Gore went on to beat R. F. Doherty in the challenge round. "R.F." was certainly in a poor state of health and his defeat came as no surprise to his friends, but Gore was a grand little player with the courage of a lion. Like S. H. Smith he was a one-stroke player, his severe and accurate forehand from the baseline being virtually his only stroke. But with that and his great endurance and pertinacity he won the Wimbledon singles championship three times.

In 1902 H. L. Doherty(3) took over the mantle discarded by his elder brother and started a run of five consecutive singles championships. But in this year the sequence of five doubles championships by the Doherty brothers was broken by the formidable but unorthodox combination of S. H. Smith and F. L. Riseley. This couple played the old fashioned one up and one back formation—Smith racing about the back of the court and crashing in his devastating forehand drives and Riseley volleying and smashing with crushing brilliance at the net. Smith and Riseley were a constant menace to the smooth working Doherty machine. They beat the wonderful brothers on the Riviera and again at Wimbledon

5 A. W. Gore at the start of his powerful forehand drive. He won the Wimbledon singles in 1901, 1908 and again in 1909 when he was 41 years of age

4 Mrs. Sterry, who won the Wimbledon singles in 1901 and 1908

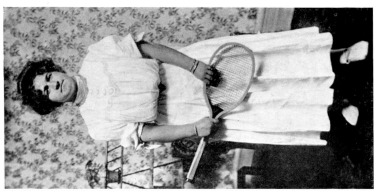

7 Miss Lottie Dod, who won Wimbledon first in 1887 at the age of 15

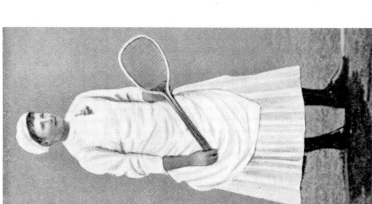
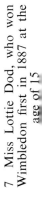

8 Miss May Sutton (U.S.A.), Wimbledon champion in 1905 and 1907

6 Mrs. Lambert Chambers who, between 1905 and 1914, won the Wimbledon singles seven times

in 1906, in what proved to be the Dohertys' last appearance on the Centre Court. But from 1903 to 1905 the Dohertys' doubles combination reigned supreme.

The Davis Cup had been won for England from America by the Dohertys in 1903. In 1905 the Americans began their challenge for world lawn tennis honours, and with the advent also of Norman Brookes(9), the Australian wizard, public interest quickened and the international flavour of Wimbledon became intensified. Brookes was undoubtedly one of the truly great players of all time. He was a left-hander of wiry, but not robust, physique and his game was packed with brains and purpose. His deceptive breaking service formed the spearhead for a persistent volleying attack which wore down the stoutest defences. As was anticipated, Brookes came through to meet H. L. Doherty in the challenge round. It was "Little Do" 's supreme test, and he came through it magnificently in three straight sets. It must be admitted, however, that the terrific struggle Brookes had had to defeat S. H. Smith in the final of the All-comers took a great deal out of him. The advantage the holder had in standing out until the challenge round was here seen demonstrated. However, this victory enhanced "H.L." 's reputation enormously and he followed it up by some great victories against the Americans in the Davis Cup.

The last Doherty Wimbledon, that of 1906, was from the point of view of the numbers of the spectators the most successful up to date. But the play was somewhat of an anti-climax after the thrills of the overseas invasion of the year before. That very fine player, and magnificent athlete and sportsman, Frank Riseley, excelled himself by first beating the only American invader, R. D. Little, and then those two stalwarts, S. H. Smith and A. W. Gore. In the challenge round Riseley took a set off H. L. Doherty.

But it was the challenge round of the doubles which provided one of the most thrilling contests ever seen at Wimbledon. The Dohertys had played Smith and Riseley four times in the championships. The latter pair had won in 1902, but the Dohertys had beaten them the three following years. This fifth meeting was a battle of giants with Frank Riseley playing an inspired game at the net whilst Smith supported him magnificently by his fierce driving from the back of the court. They were irresistible, and the smooth Doherty machine faltered and went down to defeat.

Few of those who cheered the winners and losers as they left the Centre Court after this magnificent match could have had any idea that they had witnessed the swan-song of the famous Doherty brothers. Yet they never played at Wimbledon again. They had won between them seventeen championships, in singles and doubles, in ten years. By their courteous behaviour on court, their skill, their good looks and their sportsmanship, they had given a great uplift to the game of lawn tennis all over the world. Although Britain was again to have her triumphs a quarter of a century later, her star was never again quite so bright as in the days of the magnificent Doherty brothers.

The Dohertys were such a great attraction during the years of their supremacy that they somewhat naturally put women's tennis in the shade, and the feminine championship game was still confined to singles. But there were four outstanding women players during this period—firstly Mrs. Hillyard and Mrs. Sterry and later Mrs. Lambert Chambers and the American, Miss May Sutton, who later became Mrs. Bundy. Mrs. Hillyard, who won her first championship in 1886 as Miss Bingley, was a fine runner and high jumper and became a dominating lawn tennis player on the courts of England, Ireland and the Continent. She was defeated, however, at Wimbledon the next year by the brilliant Miss Lottie Dod. Mrs. Hillyard regained the championship in Miss Dod's absence in 1889, and when Miss Dod retired in 1894, she became champion for the third time. During the next seven years she and her great rival, Miss Cooper, afterwards Mrs. Sterry(4), led the field of women's tennis—Mrs. Hillyard winning, in all, six championships and Mrs. Sterry five.

In the sphere of women's tennis particular mention must also be made of that fine Irish player, Miss L. Martin, who, between 1889 and 1903, won her own championship nine times and three times reached the final of the All-comers at Wimbledon.

In 1903 the ladies' championship at Wimbledon was won

by Miss D. K. Douglass, afterwards Mrs. Lambert Chambers (6), who was destined to win it seven times, a record only beaten by Mrs. Helen Wills-Moody. Miss Douglass was certainly a most formidable and determined match player. Her game, based on steady and accurate driving, was utterly sound and it was backed by generalship and tactics of a high order. From 1903 to 1914 she never lost at Wimbledon to any English player. In 1905, however, she lost her title to an eighteen-year-old American girl, Miss May Sutton, who was making her first visit to Wimbledon (8). Few more popular and determined personalities have ever appeared on the Centre Court. Her chief weapon was a formidable topspin forehand drive which she hit with all her force. Though rather heavily built Miss Sutton was extremely active and her charming smile and wholehearted play won all hearts. But Miss Douglass returned to the attack and had her revenge on Miss Sutton in 1906. Miss Sutton was, however, in irresistible form in 1907 and defeated Mrs. Lambert Chambers (as Miss Douglass had by this time become) quite easily. In 1903 Mrs. Sterry regained the ladies' championship after an interval of seven years—a really great performance.

With the departure of the Dohertys, and also of those other two great British stalwarts, S. H. Smith and F. L. Riseley, the British defences were weakened and for the first time all three championships were won by overseas players. The great Australian, Norman Brookes (9), had delivered a stern challenge to H. L. Doherty in 1905; in 1907 he was a better player and there was no "H.L." to stand in his way. He had reduced the break of his service, increased its speed and improved its length. His volleying was more subtle and deadly and he now established himself as one of the really great players in the history of the game. Nevertheless his passage to the championship was by no means easy. His Australasian compatriot, Anthony Wilding, took him to five sets in the second round, and Karl Behr of the U.S.A. came near to beating him in the fourth. Having beaten Gore easily in the final of the All-comers Brookes had a walk-over in the challenge round as Laurie Doherty did not defend. Brookes, though of wiry rather than robust physique, was a fine all-round athlete being first-class both at cricket and golf. Later, as Sir Norman, he was to become a great personage in Australian and world lawn tennis circles. Paired with Tony Wilding, Brookes also won the doubles, again without having to play the challenge round, as the Dohertys did not defend.

For thirty years no one but a British player had won the men's singles title at Wimbledon. In the next thirty years it was only to be secured five times by a home player. It was also curious that the year which witnessed the loss by Britain of all three championships was the first year in which the Royal Family honoured Wimbledon by their presence. The Prince of Wales (afterwards King George V) and the Princess watched the challenge round of the ladies' singles, won for the second time by the hard-hitting American girl, Miss May Sutton. The Prince subsequently accepted the presidency of the All-England Club and presented a handsome challenge cup for the men's singles.

Although 1907 marked the first visit of the Prince and Princess it was by no means their last, and they were to have the satisfaction twenty-seven years later, as King and Queen, of seeing the two singles championships once again won by British players, F. J. Perry and Miss Dorothy Round.

In the absence of Norman Brookes, that gallant British veteran, A. W. Gore, then over forty years of age, won the singles for the second time in 1908 and held his championship again in 1909.

For the next five years, until the outbreak of war in 1914, Australasia (the combination in those days of Australia and New Zealand) became the premier lawn tennis nation of the world. Wilding won the Wimbledon singles four years running, and then lost his title to Brookes in 1914(11), in which year Brookes and Wilding also won the Wimbledon doubles. From 1907 to 1911 Australasia held the Davis Cup and regained it again on the eve of the outbreak of war.

The New Zealander, Tony Wilding(11), captured the Wimbledon singles title first from the holder A. W. Gore in 1910. He defended it successfully against the challenges of H. Roper Barrett in 1911, A. W. Gore again in 1912, and the dynamic American M. A. McLoughlin in 1913. Wilding also won the Wimbledon doubles with the famous Australian,

10 Maurice E. McLoughlin (U.S.A.), "the Californian Comet", American champion 1911–13

9 Norman E. Brookes, the Australian wizard, whom Tilden considered the greatest match player the game has ever known

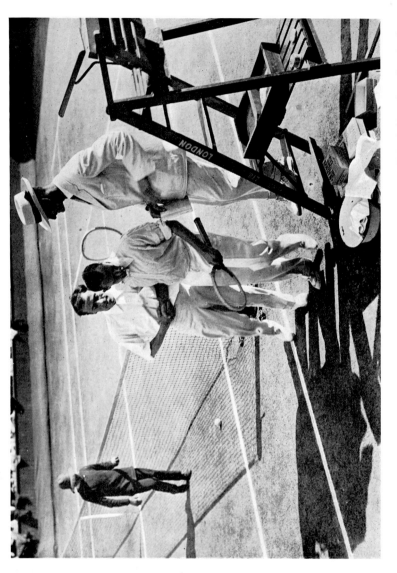

11   The last Wimbledon before World War I.   N. E. Brookes (Australia) (*left*), takes the singles title from Anthony Wilding (New Zealand), 6–4, 6–4, 7–5

Norman Brookes, in 1907, with M. J. G. Ritchie in 1908 and 1910 and again with Norman Brookes in 1914. The story of his fine achievements in the lawn tennis world is one of great endeavour, great sportsmanship and systematic training. He was indeed a very great ornament to the game he loved. There have been many more brilliant players and tacticians than Wilding, but no finer athlete has ever stepped on to the Centre Court. He believed that a first-class lawn tennis player needed to be as fit as a champion boxer, and skipping and ball punching always formed part of his training régime. Indeed, in this respect he was the forerunner of the present day Australian players, Sedgman, McGregor, Mervyn Rose, Hoad and Rosewall who, under the direction of that very great trainer and captain, Harry Hopman, have subjected themselves to a system of rigorous physical training of almost unprecedented severity in the game of lawn tennis. Many is the match which Wilding won because of his wonderful physical condition. And combined with his fine physique he had a steadfastness and toughness of mind and character which contributed greatly to his success.

Like Frank Sedgman today, Wilding throve on a great deal of play and was possibly handicapped if anything by the rule which appertained at Wimbledon in his day of the holder not playing through.

In 1914 he lost the championship he had held with such distinction for four years, but he took his defeat—bitter though it must have been—with the perfect composure and sportsmanship one would have expected of him. On May 9th, 1915, near Neuve Chapelle in France, he was killed by a shell which landed directly on his dug-out—actually within a few yards of where I was standing at the time. Many people thought that, had he been spared, he would again have won Wimbledon in 1919. But he would by then have been thirty-six and with the four years gap of the war years it would have been difficult for him to attain that pitch of physical perfection which was such an essential factor of his game. Certainly no greater sportsman and few more popular personalities have ever appeared at Wimbledon.

Wilding had made five bids at the Wimbledon Championship before success crowned his efforts in 1910. In this year no less than ninety-two players were drawn in the championship singles, and Wilding had some stern opposition to overcome. He dropped a set in the first round to that very clever British player, Roper Barrett, who had beaten him badly in 1908; dropped another set to Ritchie in the third round; and then beat the strong German player, O. Froitzheim, and the Irish international, J. C. Parke, with comparative ease. In the final of the All-comers Wilding met the American, Beals Wright, the left-handed volleying genius who had beaten him two years previously in the Davis Cup at Melbourne. The American won the first two sets, but Wilding's magnificent physical condition brought him through to victory in the fifth set. The gallant veteran, A. W. Gore, managed to win a set in the challenge round, but could do no more. Wilding was the first New Zealander to win fame at Wimbledon and his success evoked the greatest enthusiasm in the Dominion.

In the women's event Mrs. Lambert Chambers returned to the attack and gained a conclusive victory.

The 1911 Wimbledon was remarkable for the fact that there was a record field of 104 players for the men's singles, and they were representative of seventeen different nations. The pertinacious Roper Barrett came through the All-comers after a tremendous match with C. P. Dixon in the final. The challenge round was played on an intensely hot day with the enclosed Centre Court at the old Wimbledon rather resembling a furnace. Barrett, who had a bad arm, played a very brainy game nearly reducing Wilding to complete exhaustion. Instead of driving the ball he alternated soft half court strokes with wicked drop shots and lobs, making the holder race all over the court. But at two sets all Barrett, who had had to play through an exhausting Wimbledon and had not the physique of Wilding, was himself exhausted and forced to retire.

For the first time France won a Wimbledon Championship, and the play of their winning doubles pair, A. H. Gobert and Max Decugis, was a revelation in crashing services and smashes and thrusting volleying. The French pair had a tremendous battle with the German combination of Rahe and Kleinschroth in an early round, and then in the challenge round inflicted on Wilding and Ritchie their first defeat.

Mrs. Lambert Chambers inflicted a crushing defeat on Miss D. Boothby by 6–0, 6–0 and established herself as without any doubt the finest woman player in the world.

In 1912 it was generally expected that the brilliant but somewhat temperamental young French star, A. H. Gobert, who had beaten Wilding on wood in the Covered Court Championships at Queen's Club only a month previously, would come through to the Wimbledon challenge round. But Gobert was never quite so dangerous on grass, and in the final of the All-comers he went down to the evergreen veteran A. W. Gore, who was then aged forty-four. This was a really wonderful effort of Gore's against a man half his age, who only a couple of months earlier had won the Olympic gold medal in a strong field at Stockholm. Gore took a set from Wilding in the challenge round, but that was really his swan-song.

Mrs. Lambert Chambers did not defend her women's title, which was won by Mrs. Larcombe, one of the cleverest tacticians and finest volleyers in the history of women's tennis.

In 1913 America delivered yet another strong challenge at Wimbledon through her fiery champion, M. E. McLoughlin (10). He had created a great sensation in his own country when he won the American championship in 1912, and at Wimbledon, on his first and only appearance, he won equal popularity and fame. Tall and powerful, with a flaming mop of red hair, the young American champion, with his sunny smile and devastating strokes, was a tremendous draw. When he faced the wily Roper Barrett on the first day there was an unprecedented crowd at Wimbledon, and hundreds of people were turned away from the gates. And what a narrow squeak the young American had! No one could have handled his powerful service with greater skill than Barrett, nor shown more resource and guile against his devastating net attack. Eventually McLoughlin just edged out the winner, but only after the first set had been taken to vantage games. There-after the winner's passage to the challenge round was fairly comfortable, no one else being able to cope with the American's deadly service.

The stands were absolutely packed and there was a big

attendance of Americans, most of them with small stars and stripes flags, for the challenge round. Curiously enough McLoughlin was made a slight favourite, although Wilding had beaten him by three sets to one at Sydney at their last meeting—but that was four years back and the American had matured considerably since then. Wilding was in perfect physical condition for this match and his nerves and his strokes were under complete control. The deciding factors were Wilding's ability to take the powerful service of his opponent and his astuteness in pounding the American's relatively weaker backhand. Wilding won 8–6, 6–3, 10–8, but not until the last ball had bounced twice did McLoughlin cease for one moment to put his all into the struggle. It was the highlight of Wilding's career and the greatest match he had ever played. McLoughlin won the American championship that year for the second time, and then in the 1914 Davis Cup challenge round, played at New York in August, beat both Norman Brookes and Wilding—although Australasia managed to win back the Cup by three matches to two.

At the 1913 Wimbledon Mrs. Lambert Chambers won again for the sixth time, not losing a single set in any match. The holder, Mrs. Larcombe, was compelled to withdraw as, in the final of the mixed doubles, playing with J. C. Parke against Hope Crisp and Mrs. C. O. Tuckey, she was hit in the eye by a ball and put out of action for several weeks.

In the men's doubles the German pair of Rahe and Kleinschroth delivered a most spirited challenge to win the All-comers, but in the challenge round the skill and finesse of the holders, Roper Barrett and C. P. Dixon, were too much for them. In the school of tactics, and of finesse without force, there has probably never been a better men's doubles pair than Barrett and Dixon.

The 1914 Wimbledon was remarkable for the return of Norman Brookes, the champion of 1907, after an absence of seven years, and, with no Americans in the field, it appeared certain that he would come through to the final and challenge the New Zealander, Anthony Wilding. Brookes certainly started off sensationally by beating L. F. Davin, a good young Scottish player, in three love sets. And, more

12   The brothers William and Ernest Renshaw, who dominated the game
all through the 'eighties and laid the foundations of the strokes and tactics
of the modern game

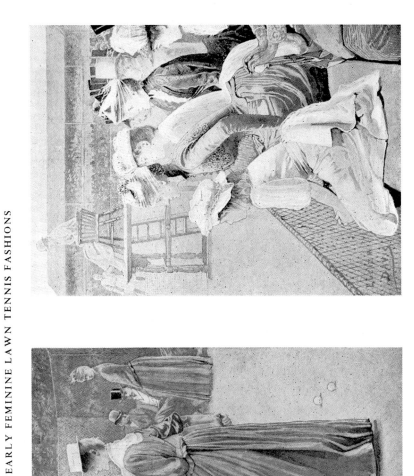

14   Watching the play at Wimbledon

13   Garden party tennis

remarkable still, he very nearly repeated the process against that fine British player, M. J. G. Ritchie, who only managed to secure two games. But in the final of the All-comers the German champion, Otto Froitzheim, almost brought about the Australian wizard's downfall. Physical stamina had never been Brookes's strong point, and his persistent net attack and breaking service took a good deal out of him. Against Froitzheim he pressed his attack from the start, obviously trying to achieve victory in three straight sets. He very nearly did so and actually led 5–4 in the third set, having won the first two. But the German gallantly saved this set and then won the fourth with Brookes wilting visibly in the close atmosphere of a particularly hot day. Both players were then quite exhausted and did in fact take a considerable rest before starting the final set. With the aid of a certain amount of luck—and some champagne at the critical moment—Brookes just nosed out a winner at 8–6. He then had another stroke of luck in that heavy rain fell on the day the challenge round should have been played and he had two clear days to recover before playing Wilding.

There have been many theories and explanations for Wilding's three-set defeat. There was no doubt that the challenger played a masterly game imposing both his strokes and his will on the holder. Needless to say Wilding, the perfect sportsman, made no excuses for his defeat by a man who, though seven years his senior, he considered to be a greater player even than the Dohertys. But Wilding really reached his zenith in 1913. He was then thirty, which would have been considered rather elderly for a champion tennis player by modern standards, and he had had a very full tennis career. In 1914 he was noticeably neither so keen nor so physically fit as he had been previously. He was eager to play through the singles event and had he been allowed to do so he might have been sharper and in better shape for the challenge round.

The ladies' challenge round followed immediately, with the Centre Court rather like a furnace. Mrs. Larcombe, the 1912 champion, came through to challenge Mrs. Lambert Chambers, but the latter just had the better of two hard-fought sets and registered her seventh singles championship, which remained as a record until broken twenty-four years later by Mrs. Helen Wills-Moody.

The ladies' doubles event, which had only been started in 1913, was won by Miss Ryan and Miss Morton—that very great doubles player, Miss Ryan, thus notching the first of her many doubles victories at Wimbledon. The other new event, the mixed doubles, was won by J. C. Parke and Mrs. Larcombe, who thus had some compensation for their bad luck the previous year.

In the men's doubles Norman Brookes and Wilding just managed to beat the holders, Roper Barrett and Dixon, in a hard-fought match.

So, with the coming of war, ended this first era of the new game of lawn tennis. In its first forty years it had progressed enormously, both in public popularity and in the skill and keenness of the players. Based first and foremost on Wimbledon, it had become a world game and could stake its claim even then as the most international of all games. For several years before 1914 it had become evident that the Worple Road Wimbledon had become too small and the accommodation for spectators quite inadequate. Only the opening of the First World War postponed its move to roomier quarters.

Looking back on this first period of the game's history it is interesting to try to pick out the most outstanding players both in singles and doubles. In doing so I will not go farther back than the Doherty era because, great champions as were the Renshaws, H. F. Lawford and their contemporaries, the game was still very much in its infancy for the first twenty years of its Wimbledon life. With the coming of the Dohertys the tempo changed and interest and competition increased to a marked extent. These then are my leading world players on all surfaces between 1897 and 1914:

MEN'S SINGLES

1. H. L. Doherty
   Great Britain
2. N. E. Brookes   Australia
3. R. F. Doherty
   Great Britain
4. A. F. Wilding New Zealand
5. M. E. McLoughlin   U.S.A.
6. A. W. Gore   Great Britain
7. A. H. Gobert   France
8. O. Froitzheim   Germany
9. S. H. Smith   Great Britain

~ 56 ~

Others who might well claim inclusion in this list are: Roper
Barrett, F. L. Riseley and C. P. Dixon of Great Britain and
Beals Wright and R. N. Williams of the U.S.A.

LADIES' SINGLES

1. Mrs. Lambert Chambers   4. Mrs. Sterry   Great Britain
       Great Britain   5. Miss Martin   Ireland
2. Miss May Sutton   U.S.A.   6. Mrs. Larcombe
3. Mrs. Hillyard   Great Britain   Great Britain

MEN'S DOUBLES

1. R. F. and H. L. Doherty	Great Britain
2. S. H. Smith and F. L. Riseley	Great Britain
3. N. E. Brookes and A. F. Wilding	Australasia
4. H. H. Hackett and F. B. Alexander	U.S.A.
5. H. Roper Barrett and C. P. Dixon	Great Britain
6. M. E. McLoughlin and H. H. Hackett	U.S.A.
7. N. E. Brookes and A. W. Dunlop	Australasia
8. B. C. Wright and K. Behr	U.S.A.
9. S. N. Doust and A. B. Jones	Australasia
10. A. F. Wilding and M. J. G. Ritchie	Great Britain
11. H. Ward and B. C. Wright	U.S.A.
12. A. H. Gobert and M. Decugis	France

The pastime of picking "the greatest ever" at any sport is
always a fascinating one. Others may well place my selections
in a different order or replace some of them altogether. In a
later chapter I shall attempt to compare the different periods
and arrive at a greatest ever list from them all.

Chapter Three

THE INTER-WAR
YEARS

WITH A LONG SIGH of relief a war-weary world turned its thoughts to peace, and it was only natural that people should seek an outlet in sport. The war of 1914–18 took a far greater toll of our young men than did the war of 1939–45, although the actual physical damage to Britain in the First World War was infinitesimal compared with the second. The war had started in 1914 with Australasia as the leading lawn tennis nation. They were the holders of the Davis Cup, Norman Brookes held the Wimbledon singles title, and Brookes and Wilding the doubles. But Brookes was now getting on in years, as lawn tennis champions go, and Wilding had been killed in the war. In Britain and on the Continent the game had been in almost complete abeyance for four years. America, however, who had come late into the war, had continued her national championships all through the war years, with the exception of 1917.

A great little champion had arisen in 1915 in W. M. Johnston, generally known as "Little Bill" to distinguish him from another coming champion, W. T. Tilden, known as "Big Bill". Another brilliant player, R. N. Williams, who won the American title in 1914 and 1916, had arisen during the war years and had resisted the further challenges of dynamic red-headed Maurice McLoughlin to attain national honours. Up to this time the United States had never succeeded in winning a Wimbledon men's singles or doubles championship, but even before the war their challenge was becoming stronger, and, in the conditions which appertained

15 "The Two Helens." Mrs. Helen Wills-Moody (*left*), and Miss Helen Jacobs—both of U.S.A.

16 Miss Dorothy Round (G.B.), Wimbledon champion 1934 and 1937

17 Miss Betty Nuthall, the only Englishwoman to win the American championships (1930)

18 Past Wimbledon champions awaiting the presentatic

19 Mr. and Mrs.
Godfree (*left*), the only
married couple ever to
win the mixed doubles
at Wimbledon (1926),
and Miss Colyer

heir Jubilee medals by the King and Queen in 1926

20 The two greatest women players, Mlle Suzanne Lenglen (*left*) and her successor Mrs. Helen Wills-Moody

21 "Big Bill" Tilden (U.S.A.) winning the singles at Wimbledon in 1930

when the war ended, a Wimbledon championship appeared to be theirs for the taking.

But, as far as the men's events were concerned, the first post-war Wimbledon started on a somewhat low note. The entry for the men's singles was certainly a record, but there were representatives of only eight overseas nations—and the formidable Americans were absent. The entry list bristled with great names, but the play was, rather naturally, well below the pre-war standard. They were "either too young or too old", in the words of a popular music-hall song. A tall vigorous young Australian, Gerald Patterson, with obvious limitations but with a murderous service and smash, a powerful forehand, and a somewhat awkwardly produced and vulnerable backhand, swept all before him. He lost only one set, to M. J. G. Ritchie, and in the final overcame A. R. F. Kingscote, who had survived three long and tough consecutive matches. The great Australian, Norman Brookes, came over to defend his title, but, now nearing forty years of age and obviously in nothing like his 1914 form, the wizard had to bow to the virile attack of his young compatriot.

But exciting as was the play of Gerald Patterson, all the thunder of the first post-war Wimbledon was stolen by a young French girl, Mlle Suzanne Lenglen (18, 20), who came, saw and conquered at her first attempt. And the whole world of women's tennis was to revolve around her until she retired from the amateur game six years later. Mlle Lenglen was the first and only Frenchwoman to win the Wimbledon singles title. Born at Compiègne in 1899, she was just twenty when she came to Wimbledon. But, although the high standard of her play was a surprise to British lawn tennis, she had been well known on the Continent for some years. At the age of fourteen she had been beating everyone in Riviera tournaments, and in 1913, at Cannes, she had put up strong resistance to the great Mrs. Lambert Chambers herself. At the age of fifteen she had won the hard-court championship of the world at St. Cloud, and, had it not been for the war, she might well have started winning at Wimbledon earlier than she did.

Suzanne Lenglen owed everything to her father, no great player himself, who had coached, trained and encouraged her from her very earliest days. The saying "Il faut souffrir pour être belle" can be applied equally well to the ground-work which must be undertaken by anyone who aspires to become a great lawn tennis player. An infinite capacity for taking pains may or may not be the criterion of a genius, but it has made many a tennis champion, and indeed I have never known one who did not possess that quality. But not even Bill Tilden, his own severest critic and taskmaster, ever toiled and practised so hard as did Suzanne under the martinet direction of her father.

She possessed, of course, certain invaluable initial qualifi-cations. She had natural grace and co-ordination of move-ment, a good eye, a strong and wiry body and a phenomenal amount of nervous energy, without which no athlete will reach the heights. All these natural qualities were deliberately developed by her father in her early training, and were increased by her actual match play experience. But, as time went on, she drew so lavishly on her nervous energy that it burnt up her physical resources and destroyed the balance of a perfect machine. Having given her the tools for the job in the shape of adequate strokes, Monsieur Lenglen put his pupil through a practice régime of merciless severity designed to enable her to put the ball on a sixpence wherever she willed. It was this deadly accuracy, coupled with her ease and swiftness of movement, which formed the basis of her overwhelming success.

In 1919 her game had not attained its full strength, nor had she herself reached the pinnacle of her confidence and poise. But from her first match, which she won for the loss of only one game, crowds flocked to watch her play. So much was this so that it became an embarrassment to the referee who, unable to keep the crowds on the outside courts in check, had to put almost all her matches on the Centre Court. In the second round that very good player, Mrs. Larcombe, the 1912 champion, could only get three games from Suzanne. She lost but one game to Mrs. Craddock in the third round, and then met Miss K. McKane, the most promising young player in Britain. But one game was all that Miss McKane could win.

In the semi-final Mlle Lenglen met Miss Elizabeth Ryan, a

Californian who had been resident in England since 1912. Miss Ryan, with her vicious chopped forehand, sizzling volleys, strong physique and great determination, was a stern test for anyone. She had come through to the final of the All-comers in 1914 and was indeed probably the best woman player who never won a Wimbledon singles championship. Suzanne won the first set 6–4, and led 5–2 and 40–15 in the second. But Miss Ryan put in a great counter-attack which shook the highly strung French girl to the core. Miss Ryan drew level at 5–5 and few would have given much for Suzanne's chances. But a rain storm which delayed play for an hour gave her a breathing space and she ran out a winner at 7–5.

This brought her to the final of the All-comers against Mrs. Satterthwaite, to whom she conceded only two games.

The challenge round, in which Suzanne opposed the renowned Mrs. Lambert Chambers, seven times Wimbledon champion, is generally considered to have been the greatest and most exciting women's single in the whole history of the game of lawn tennis. I think it was; and no one who saw that historic match will ever forget it. It had been arranged for the Friday of the second week of Wimbledon. All that day the players, and the huge crowd which had assembled, watched the rain falling in a steady downpour until it was decided that no play was possible. However, when the players came on to court next day, with King George V, Queen Mary and Princess Mary amongst the spectators, they gave no sign of the nervous strain they must have been suffering. The playing conditions were perfect, and both players were keyed up to give of their best; the holder, Mrs. Lambert Chambers, who, sixteen years before, had won the first of her seven Wimbledon singles championships, and the young French challenger, who was appearing at Wimbledon for the first time. The latter's wonderful succession of victories in her progress to the challenge round and her great advantage in age had made her a firm favourite for the title. Yet on a hot day the determined and experienced Mrs. Lambert Chambers was actually twice within a stroke of victory. After a terrific struggle the French girl took the first set at 10–8. But the holder never flinched nor wilted, and when she squared the match by winning the second set at 6–4 it looked as though she would win after all. Suzanne looked the more exhausted and had to be revived with brandy. The final set was a ding-dong struggle played in an atmosphere of mounting excitement. First Suzanne forged ahead, but was caught and passed by Mrs. Chambers, who reached 6–5 and 40–15, thus having two match points. Chancing her luck on an all-out offensive Suzanne saved the first match point with a lucky volley off the wood of her racket. An error by Mrs. Chambers lost her the second—and with it her last real chance had gone. Keeping her nerves under wonderful control, Mlle Lenglen went out at 9–7 to win a brilliant and memorable victory.

In the same year she won the first of six doubles victories in partnership with Miss Ryan.

Nineteen-twenty was an historic year at Wimbledon in that it marked the first American victory in the men's singles. Hitherto the high-water mark of their endeavours had been Maurice McLoughlin's success in the All-comers in 1913. This year they sent over a strong team, headed by their champion, W. M. Johnston, and his closest rival, W. T. Tilden(21). Johnston was unexpectedly beaten in the second round by the Irish rugger and tennis international, J. C. Parke, who went out to Tilden in the next round. In his next round, however, Tilden only survived by the skin of his teeth a tremendous five-set match with that fine British player, A. R. F. Kingscote, who was just about Britain's best player in the years immediately after the First World War. In the final of the All-comers, Tilden met the Japanese champion, Z. Shimizu, and won in three sets. It was generally anticipated that the challenge round between the Australian holder, Gerald Patterson, and W. T. Tilden would be a very close match. But Tilden, having lost the first set in probing his opponent's defences, found a glaring weakness in Patterson's awkwardly produced backhand; and having discovered the weakness he peppered it unmercifully, using a heavily sliced shot which could not have been more difficult for the Australian. The further the match went, the more pronounced Tilden's superiority became, and he eventually won in four sets. Tilden had arrived as one of the most vivid personalities,

22, 23 and 24 The famous "Four Musketeers" of France, supreme at Wimbledon from 1924 to 1929. *Above* (*left to right*) Jean Borotra, Henri Cochet and René Lacoste. *Below* "Toto" Brugnon and Jean Borotra, "the bounding Basque"

26   A British stylist, H. W. Austin,
Wimbledon finalist in 1932

25   F. J. Perry (*left*), Britain's great champion and winner of
three consecutive Wimbledon singles titles from 1934 to 1936,

and possibly the finest player, the game has ever seen. Very tall, with an attractive smile and a completely confident manner, he could generally be seen strolling through an admiring crowd in the long woolly sweaters of various hues which he affected. Armed with a fine physique, every shot in the game, a keen tennis brain and a great fighting spirit, he was indeed a very worthy champion. For six long years of constant play Tilden was unbeaten in a championship or Davis Cup match—a really wonderful record. For six successive years, 1920–25, he won the championship of the United States, and during that time he fought fifteen Davis Cup singles battles without a defeat. Wimbledon never saw Tilden at his best. He had not reached the peak of his game when he scored his first two victories in 1920 and 1921, despite the fact that he was twenty-seven when he achieved his first Wimbledon championship—for he was born in February, 1893. When he came to Wimbledon again in 1927 he was thirty-four—a veteran age for any other tennis player but Tilden.

He started playing tennis at the early age of fourteen, and from the beginning he was obviously endowed with all the qualities necessary for a champion. His telescopic reach, enormous stride, steely physique, inexhaustible stamina and natural eye for a ball were all marvellous assets. And on top of that he had great tennis wisdom, the priceless ability to stand outside himself and criticise his own strokes with an impartial eye. Nothing but the best was ever good enough for him, and there was no stroke he was content not to master. His whole game was build on speed—speed of movement about the court and speed of stroke. Not that he did not possess the more delicate strokes as well. He had an exquisite drop shot, and was a complete master of every type of spin. I have always thought that the very variety of his strokes was in one sense a handicap to him. Just as a golf player with a bag of many clubs may sometimes be in a dilemma as to which he should use, so the lawn tennis player with many strokes at his command may hesitate just that fatal split second over his choice. This was noticeable later in his career when he had to face the great little Frenchman, Henri Cochet, a man of singularly few strokes and whose game was essentially simple and uncomplicated. Tilden and Suzanne Lenglen, probably the greatest players of their respective sexes who have ever lived, had much in common. They were both masters of their craft and they both perfected their game by infinite study and practice. Suzanne was no theorist or critic of her own strokes. Her father did all that for her. But Tilden was his own tutor and critic, and his journey to the top of the world of lawn tennis is an object lesson for every aspirant to fame. He started as a rather wild hitter—and indeed I have hardly ever known a great player who started as a soft player—cultivated speed, and then acquired control. By the end of the war and the start of full competition he was high up on the American lawn tennis ladder, and in 1918 was runner-up in the American Championships. But in the final of those championships in 1919 he was crushed by W. M. Johnston in straight sets. Johnston concentrated all his artillery on Tilden's weak backhand. It is a very hard thing for a player who has reached championship class to go into obscurity and entirely remodel one of his strokes. But Tilden realised that without a topspin backhand drive in his bag he would never climb to the top of the world's lawn tennis ladder. So in months of laborious and back-breaking practice he taught himself a new backhand. And the resulting improvement in his game was immediately apparent.

In 1923 came a further milestone in his lawn tennis development. He cut his finger on the back-stop netting; blood poisoning set in, and the top of the middle finger of his right (racket) hand had to be amputated. For any ordinary man this might have spelled the end of his championship career. But Tilden turned the accident to his own advantage. It forced him to cultivate more aggression and more speed to overcome the slight weakness of grip. And once again out of weakness came additional strength.

Tilden was not only a great personality but a great showman. He never played a dull match, and he managed to dramatise or burlesque any game he played. He was always surrounded by a group of boys whom he was in process of converting into lawn tennis prodigies. But although Tilden understood the theory of the game perfectly and could apply his theories to his own game, very few of his protégés ever did much good. An outstanding exception was Vincent Richards, who showed a natural aptitude for the game from his very early days and would have been a champion in any case. It is a curious fact that very few of the great players have been good teachers.

I don't want to make out that Tilden was a lawn tennis paragon. He had none of the Doherty modesty and charm. He was a terror to linesmen and ball-boys, and often showed off on court in a most outrageous manner. The sad end to his career is public property—but that has nothing to do with lawn tennis. In 1920 and 1921, when he won the last two championships of the old Wimbledon, Tilden and Suzanne Lenglen between them caused such a sensation and drew such enormous crowds that lawn tennis leapt still further forward in the eyes of the public as a great world sport.

The ladies' singles in 1920 did not attract a very large overseas entry, but Mrs. Mallory, the new American champion, who had succeeded Mrs. Wightman, was competing. She could, however, only win three games from Mrs. Lambert Chambers, who returned to get her revenge from Suzanne Lenglen. Mrs. Lambert Chambers duly came through to the challenge round after an easy victory over Miss Ryan. Fourteen years before Mrs. Lambert Chambers had returned to challenge and beat her former conqueror, Miss May Sutton. Some thought history might repeat itself. But this time it was not to be. Mlle Lenglen, with many years of youth on her side, had now become the complete player. She overwhelmed her challenger by 6–3, 6–0. This was the last singles match Mrs. Lambert Chambers ever played at Wimbledon.

This year Mlle Lenglen secured the triple crown, winning her second victory with Miss Ryan in the women's doubles, and taking the mixed with Gerald Patterson.

Nineteen twenty-one was the last championship at the old Wimbledon, and the entry for the men's events was the greatest there had ever been. A young South African, B. I. C. Norton, surprised everyone by reaching the challenge round after tough five-set struggles with the American, F. T. Hunter, and the brilliant and colourful Spaniard, Manuel Alonso.

Norton should certainly have won the challenge round also, as Tilden had only quite recently left a nursing home and was far from fit. Norton won the first two sets, and then deliberately threw the next two away as a protest against a small section of the crowd's bad manners in barracking Tilden's drop shots. In the final set Norton had two match points but failed to clinch a thoroughly unsatisfactory and altogether unworthy championship. Mlle Lenglen won the singles for the third successive year, losing only two games to her challenger, Miss Elizabeth Ryan. Mlle Lenglen and Miss Ryan won the women's doubles as a matter of course. They only lost ten games in the eight sets they played. It was appropriate that the last ball on the old Centre Court at Wimbledon should have been hit by Mlle Lenglen.

The opening of the new Wimbledon by the King on June 26th, 1922, was naturally a great milestone in the game, and it coincided with the wettest fortnight in the history of the championships. Nevertheless there was a record entry, and, considering the weather, really big crowds of spectators. It was in this year that the challenge round was abolished in all three events. Mlle Lenglen, the only holder competing, was perfectly ready to play through, and, indeed, most of the players had been in favour of the new system for years. The opening match on the new Centre Court was played between two British players, A. R. F. Kingscote, Britain's leading singles player in the immediate post-war years, and L. A. Godfree. The latter served the first ball—and kept it as a memento.

G. L. Patterson of Australia regained the singles championship he had lost to Tilden in 1920, but only after tense five-set struggles with Britain's A. R. F. Kingscote and his own hard-hitting compatriot, J. O. Anderson. Three young Frenchmen, who were to become great champions in the years to come, competed this year at Wimbledon for the first time. Their names were René Lacoste, Jean Borotra and Henri Cochet.

Perhaps the surprise of the championships was the poor showing of the great Suzanne Lenglen. Not that she lost a set, of course; and indeed she defeated the American champion, Mrs. Mallory, for the loss of only two games; but she was taken to vantage games both by Miss McKane and Miss Ryan, and she seemed to have lost something of her former domination. Mlle Lenglen and Miss Ryan again won the women's doubles, and Suzanne for the second time became a triple winner when she won the mixed doubles with O'Hara Wood of Australia, a lovely volleyer and grand exponent of the doubles game. Lycett and Anderson won the men's doubles at 11–9 in the fifth set from Patterson and O'Hara Wood of Australia.

Nineteen twenty-three was W. M. Johnston's year, and he was certainly one of the most popular winners ever seen at Wimbledon. He had first won his own championship in America in 1915, and again in 1919, when he had beaten Tilden all ends up. This year his pulverising topspin forehand drive, sliced service and backhand and sizzling volleys were all working perfectly, and he had little difficulty in beating his compatriot, F. T. Hunter, in the final in 45 minutes for the loss of only four games. Johnston, with his "Western" grip and curiously long and looping preparation, could hit a forehand drive just about as hard as anyone has ever hit that stroke before or since. He was small and very light, and the pace he got on the ball was due to his perfect timing and weight control.

In the women's singles Mlle Lenglen was right back to her very best form, losing only eleven games in the fourteen sets she had to play to win the event. She seldom had to volley or leave a central position in the middle of the baseline. Her supremacy really came from the first stroke in the rally which she placed with such exact accuracy that the winning of the point, after three or four frantic stretches by her opponent, was only a matter of time—and very quick time at that.

Randolph Lycett achieved a notable performance in the men's doubles, which he won for the third year in succession, and with a different partner each time. There have been few better doubles players in the game's history. Had he been able to find one partner who suited him they would have made a devastating pair. This year he won with a British player, L. A. Godfree(19). Lycett also won the mixed doubles with Miss Ryan for the third time, and there have been few better mixed partnerships than theirs.

Mlle Lenglen and Miss Ryan won their fifth consecutive women's doubles as easily as usual, though they did have a bit of a fright in the final against two young British girls, Miss Evelyn Colyer(19) and Miss Joan Austin, who won three games in succession against the champions by an inspired volleying attack. Suzanne was visibly shaken by this onslaught, which was very naturally backed by the delighted support of the crowd. But Miss Ryan, steady and solid as always, pulled her more temperamental partner through the crisis into calmer waters.

These two colourful young British girls were affectionately known as "The Babes". Joan Austin was a sister of Bunny Austin and later married Randolph Lycett. Evelyn Colyer died tragically soon after her early marriage. Their career in championship tennis was short, but in their brief appearance on the Wimbledon stage they brought to the game a certain glamour and excitement which stirred the crowds as few other women's partnerships have done.

Lawn tennis supremacy has always gone in cycles, and 1924 was to mark the transference of premier honours from the New World to the Old. For six years France was to be supreme at Wimbledon. During those years Borotra, Cochet and Lacoste each won the championship twice. Between 1925 and 1933 French pairs won the men's doubles five times. Their three great singles players also won their own French championships nine years running between 1924 and 1932. Between 1926 and 1928 either Lacoste or Cochet won the American singles all three years, and France held the coveted Davis Cup from 1927 to 1932. What a wonderful record for any nation! No other continental nation has ever won the Davis Cup nor supplied a male singles champion at Wimbledon. The three great French singles players, with their teammate Jacques Brugnon, that doyen of doubles players, put French lawn tennis on top of the world. The torch of enthusiasm had already been lit in France by the incomparable Suzanne Lenglen, and it was carried forward by the "Four Musketeers" of France.

Brugnon(24), though he could pair equally well with either Borotra or Cochet, never rose to the same heights as the other three in the singles game. Lacoste was essentially a singles player, though he was not above winning a Wimbledon doubles championship, which he did with Borotra in 1925. Borotra and Cochet were equally good in singles and doubles, and they were so unlike, both in style and method, as to show the youth of France—and indeed of the world—that the way to the stars does not lie along any stereotyped or obvious pathway. Brugnon was the perfect accompanist who always subordinated himself to whichever of his great compatriots he was partnering.

Jean Borotra(22) was a magnificent athlete with a wonderful eye for a ball and natural reflexes. With a moderate groundstroke equipment, which included an awkwardly produced but nevertheless effective backhand, he had a strong service, crushing overhead, flashing and decisive volleys and wonderful mobility and anticipation. But it was his great determination, acute lawn tennis brain, and vivid personality, rather than his actual play which were such a great asset to France. On a wood surface Borotra was probably, in his prime, the greatest player that has ever lived.

René Lacoste(23) was a player of quite different character and methods. He was the perfect tennis machine, and by the time he was twenty-one he had won the championships of France, Britain and America. By sheer industry and an infinite capacity for taking pains, he made himself into the most efficient stroke player in the world. Of all the Four Musketeers of France, Lacoste was the most consistent and reliable—though he was not so tough physically as either Cochet or Borotra. Although Lacoste lacked personality on the court, yet his superlative play, combined with his modesty and perfect court manners, made him one of the most popular players at Wimbledon.

Henri Cochet(22) was considered by Bill Tilden to be possibly the greatest player that has ever lived. He was certainly the perfect riposte to the "big game" of his great American adversary. Cochet absorbed the speed of Tilden's game and used it, without effort, to his own advantage. Cochet was a small man with an insignificant service and an almost non-existent backhand, who by his amazing personality and sheer genius for the game defeated at one time or another all the best players of his time. No champion—

not even Fred Perry—has had fewer strokes, yet none has possessed such complete mastery of the strokes which he had. Cochet was never hurried and never worried. His perfect footwork and wonderful reflexes took him easily up to the ball, and although he had to play more fifth sets than most reigning champions, if it did come to a fifth set Cochet was rarely defeated.

In 1924 the Wimbledon authorities introduced a modified seeding of the draw which consisted in separating the nominated players of any one country, not exceeding four in number, as widely as possible away from one another. Twenty different nations were represented in the men's singles, and the entry was studded with stars. The leading American was young Vincent Richards, ranked that year as second in the world to W. T. Tilden. After winning the first set against Jean Borotra, Richards collapsed before the dynamic net attack of the "Bounding Basque". Lacoste had his hardest struggle against the Spaniard, Manuel Alonso, in the second round. In the third round Norman Brookes, the Australian wizard, scored a most remarkable five-set victory over America's F. T. Hunter, the 1923 finalist, who had been ranked as the fifth best player in the world. This victory certainly places Brookes among the immortals. He was then forty-seven years of age, and had really only come over to England on a business visit.

For the first time in Wimbledon history two Frenchmen met in the final, which was one of the shortest ever seen, though it went to the full five sets. Never could there have been a greater contrast in styles, the acrobatic brilliance of Borotra matching the soundness and certainty of Lacoste. Beneath the black beret of Jean Borotra beat a most acute tennis brain. He went all out to win the first set at 6–1, was content to lose the second quickly, launched all his artillery to win the third 6–1, and could then marshal his physical resources so that when the vital fifth set started he was fresher than his opponent. Borotra clinched his victory at 6–4.

How often have I seen Borotra adopt these selfsame tactics, and how often have I seen his adversary fall for them. It always seemed so certain that Borotra would "blow up" from the very vehemence of his own attack and that a waiting game would pay. And yet they could never see that, with the first vital set in his bag, it was Borotra who could afford to wait and arrange the last act of the play to suit his own curtain.

The players who really worried and exhausted Borotra attacked him hard from the very start and gave of their best in the first set. If Borotra failed to win the first set fairly comfortably, then indeed his lack of solid and dependable ground strokes made things very tough for him in a five-set match. In a three-set match Borotra often adopted very different tactics, and would fence with his opponent for a set, knowing that he could afford to throw in his all in the third set. It is the case with almost all lawn tennis players I have known that fatigue clouds the judgment. That is why an astute critic can often judge the finer points of a match better than the protagonists themselves. Even the great Tilden was no exception to this rule—but then he rarely found an opponent who exhausted him. But Borotra, more than any player I have known, could keep an ice-cold brain when his legs were like lead and his heart was bursting. Like a wounded tiger he was never so dangerous as when, at the end of a desperate struggle, his opponent closed in for the kill.

Borotra's win in 1924 was enormously popular with the crowd, and he remained from then on, and way into his fifties, a tremendous favourite at Wimbledon. In fact it was on British courts, on the fast green turf of the All-England Club, and on the even faster wood surface of the famous East court at Queen's Club—and he was supreme on wood—that Borotra was really more in his element, and more appreciated, than anywhere else in the world.

For the first time since the war Mlle Lenglen failed to win at least two championships. An attack of jaundice earlier in the year had pulled her down a lot, and she only survived her fourth round match against the very formidable Miss Ryan at 6–4 in the final set. She then had to scratch to Britain's best player, Miss Kitty McKane, who came through to the final to meet the eighteen-year-old American champion, Miss Helen Wills. Against all expectation, and indeed against the run of the play, Miss McKane eventually triumphed, by a great display of courage and determination, to become the first home champion since the war. But it was the worst of bad luck for Miss Ryan. Miss Wills had some consolation for her singles defeat by winning the women's doubles with her compatriot, Mrs. Wightman(50), a really great doubles player and the donor of the famous Wightman Cup.

Nineteen twenty-five was the first year that qualifying competitions were held for those would-be players at Wimbledon who failed to be accepted for one of the ordinary vacancies in the draw.

In this year the crowds at Wimbledon were bigger than ever, and on only one day did rain interfere with the play. Once again the two young Frenchmen, Jean Borotra, the holder, and twenty-one-year-old René Lacoste met in the final and King George V came down to see the match. But this year Lacoste won the first two sets, and Borotra was then always struggling and just failed to square the match in the fourth set. The phlegmatic Lacoste for once showed his feelings on court by throwing the big white cap, which he almost invariably wore, high into the air when the final point had been won. Borotra and Lacoste paired up to win the men's doubles.

Suzanne Lenglen, fully restored to health, was now at the very peak of her wonderful form. In winning the championship (for the sixth time) for the loss of only five games in all, she set up a record which will probably remain for all time. She actually beat Miss McKane, the holder, 6–0, 6–0—a quite unprecedented and amazing score for a holder to lose by—and won forty games in succession during her singles matches.

For the sixth time Mlle Lenglen won the women's doubles with Miss Ryan. In these six years they played together at Wimbledon they never lost more than fourteen games in the whole doubles event in any one year. Miss Ryan won nineteen doubles championships at Wimbledon—and with ten different partners. As a pair I would class these two as the greatest women's doubles combination of all time. By winning the mixed doubles with Jean Borotra, Mlle Lenglen gained the triple crown for the third time—another all-time record. Who could have possibly believed that she was never to win a Wimbledon championship again?

Nineteen twenty-six will always be remembered as Wimbledon's Jubilee year—the fiftieth anniversary of the first championship meeting. All the surviving champions were invited on the opening day to be presented to the King and Queen, and to receive commemorative medals(18). The ex-champions were led by P. F. Hadow, who won the singles in 1878, the second year of the championships' inception, and by Miss Maud Watson, the first lady champion of 1884–85.

In this Jubilee year it was fitting that the colourful and dynamic Jean Borotra should win the singles—after a terrific five-set match with his compatriot, Henri Cochet, in the semi-final.

But the drama of this Jubilee year was provided by Mlle Lenglen. The extent to which deference should be paid to a player of great world reputation is always a debatable point. Naturally special consideration should be given to a reigning champion, if only because vast crowds have come to see him or her play; and he or she has probably to play right through all three events. Nevertheless I am all against privileged prima donnas in sport, and I believe that the champion has a duty to her public and to her opponent, and that, within reason, the ordinary rules should apply. When the curtain goes up at a big opera or a ballet the leading man or lady must be on stage—and I believe at Wimbledon he or she must be on court. Therefore, despite my unbounded admiration for Mlle Lenglen's lawn tennis, I am one of those who support the referee, the late Mr. F. R. Burrow, in his handling of this situation.

Mlle Lenglen's great superiority over all other players had gone to her head, and the strain of remaining so supreme had got on her nerves—and she had lived on her nerves for years. On the first Wednesday of the meeting when she was due to play a single at 2 o'clock and a double at 4.30 she did not arrive until 3.30, and then became so temperamental that she left the ground without playing at all. She should, of course, have been scratched, but to scratch such a crowd-attraction would have demanded a very bold referee indeed, even though Queen Mary had come down especially to see her play. The most unusual course, possible only for a star of such magnitude, was taken in postponing both her matches until the next day and meeting her wish to play her ladies' double before her singles. For the first time in her Wimbledon career her famous doubles partnership with Miss Ryan had been broken up and she had to play with her compatriot, Mlle Vlasto. They came twice within a point of beating Miss Ryan and Miss Mary K. Browne.

But Mlle Lenglen now became too temperamental for words. In the last four days of the first week of Wimbledon she only played three of the six matches in which she was advertised to appear. She failed to turn up on the second Monday, and on the following day she retired from the tournament altogether. It was a very sad end to the career of the greatest woman tennis player of all time.

She then turned professional, but after one tour in America she returned to France and started an instructional school of lawn tennis in Paris. She died in Paris in 1938.

The women's Wimbledon singles of 1926 was won by Mrs. L. A. Godfree (Miss K. McKane), who beat the mercurial and brilliant Senorita L. de Alvarez in the final. Mrs. Godfree won the mixed doubles with her husband and they thus created an all-time record of being the only married couple to win the mixed doubles at Wimbledon(19).

The men's doubles was notable for the entry of a member of the Royal Family. H.R.H. The Duke of York—later King George VI—played in this event in partnership with Wing-Commander Louis Greig(1). They were beaten by the old champions, Gore and Roper Barrett.

For the second year running the men's doubles was won by a French pair—this time Cochet and Brugnon.

The women's doubles was won by Miss Ryan and Miss Browne, who had narrowly defeated Mlle Lenglen and Mlle Vlasto.

Nineteen twenty-seven saw the return to Wimbledon of the great Bill Tilden, who, having won the American singles six times running, had surrendered his crown to René Lacoste of France. Tilden had not visited England since he had won the Wimbledon Championship in 1921. Nineteen twenty-seven also saw the complete seeding of the draw in all events. It was one of the most thrilling and the wettest Wimbledons ever. Both Borotra and Lacoste had already become Wimbledon champions, and this year it was the turn of their very brilliant compatriot, Henri Cochet. In each match of his last three rounds he lost the first two sets. In the semi-final he met Tilden. They had met twice previously, each winning once. Tilden, in terrific form, won the first two sets 6–2, 6–4, and reached 5–1 in the third. Then came the most amazing collapse in lawn tennis history for which no one has ever provided a really satisfactory solution. It was not that Tilden's strokes or physique failed him. But Cochet seemed to impose upon him a virility of character which he could not counter—and the great Tilden wilted and went down to defeat. In the other semi-final Borotra once again met Lacoste. What a queer game tennis is! Lacoste at this time had the almost certain beating of Tilden, who was equally sure of beating Borotra. Yet Borotra knew he could probably beat Lacoste if he could only win the first two sets. This he did by the expenditure of all his physical resources. In the third and fourth sets he could only win one game in each, and he staggered about the court seemingly on the point of utter exhaustion. But in the fifth set Borotra found new reserves of strength and volleyed Lacoste off the court.

The final between Borotra and Cochet proved a most memorable affair. Once again Borotra won the first two sets, lost the next two and went to 5–2 and match point. But Cochet had the heart of a lion, and was by no means dismayed. Borotra had five more match points and Cochet won them all—and the set and match at 7–5. What a remarkable little player Cochet was—no service, no backhand, but a wonderful smash, incisive volley and a forehand which Tilden thought the best in the world. But how he made it I just don't know. I took a line for him every match he played at this Wimbledon—and still couldn't find out. It was produced by a combination of easy reflexes and perfect timing.

Miss Helen Wills, returning to Wimbledon after a two year absence, won the first of her eight singles victories, beating Lili de Alvarez in the final, as she did the following year. In 1928 Lacoste gained his second victory in a very strong field, which included five previous winners. The stylish British player, H. W. Austin, was the only one to take

Lacoste to five sets. Tilden ruined France's hopes of having four players in the semi-final by putting out Borotra, of whom he always had the beating on grass. Tilden, giving away twelve years in age, fought magnificently against the machine-like Lacoste, but couldn't quite stay the course. Cochet easily beat his young compatriot, C. Boussus, and thus came to the fourth all-French final in five years. Lacoste, this year at his very best, won fairly comfortably.

Tilden was still struggling to regain the world supremacy he had lost both at Wimbledon and Forest Hills to the brilliant French players. In 1929 he returned to Wimbledon again, where he reached the semi-final without great difficulty. An English player, H. W. Austin (26), a really beautiful player to watch, also reached the semi-final, the first Englishman to have got thus far for six years. Then Borotra beat Austin in four sets and Cochet beat Tilden in three straight sets—a most brilliant performance. Cochet won his second Wimbledon singles championship by beating Borotra comfortably in the final. I took a line in this match and marvelled at the complete mental and moral ascendancy Cochet had assumed over both Tilden and Borotra. Tilden was, of course, by now past his best, though he did regain his American championship that year, and was again to win at Wimbledon.

America had some very fine doubles combinations about this time, and one of them, Allison and van Ryn, won the event as they did the following year. They were just about as good a doubles pair as there has ever been.

Miss Helen Wills (15), now a very complete player, won the women's singles for the third time running with considerable ease. Her concentration and utter expressionless calm on court had earned for her the name of "Miss Poker-face". Her game was based on the rock of hard accurate baseline driving on either wing, as I believe a women's game must be. She "played herself in" like a good opening batsman at cricket, hitting the ball to start with well above the net and with moderate speed. Then, having got her length and timing correct, she would lower the trajectory of her driving, increase her speed, and draw right away from her opponent. Without having the genius or the wonderful touch and mobility of Lenglen she yet had a more level temperament and played a typical woman's game to perfection. She could volley and smash decisively when called upon to do so, and three times won the women's doubles at Wimbledon and once the mixed —though she never won the triple crown. In all she won eight Wimbledon singles championships—a record which may well never be beaten. She won her own American championship seven times.

The year 1930 marked the end of the long French reign at Wimbledon. No French player won again at Wimbledon— nor indeed at Forest Hills—until Y. Petra was successful in 1946; but Borotra and Brugnon managed to win the Wimbledon doubles twice together in 1932 and 1933. France, however, still retained the Davis Cup until 1933 when she lost to Great Britain.

Nineteen thirty marked the great come-back of W. T. Tilden, who regained his singles title at the age of thirty-seven —a really remarkable performance. Cochet was put out by the hard-hitting American, Wilmer Allison, and Borotra went down to Tilden in a magnificent fighting five-set battle in the semi-final. This was as good a match as Borotra ever played, but he was never quite able to beat Tilden, except on a wooden surface. Tilden beat Allison in the final in three straight sets.

Tilden never played at Wimbledon again, and shortly afterwards joined the professional ranks. And so a really great player made his bow to the world of amateur tennis.

The men's doubles was won for the second year running by that fine American team of Allison and van Ryn. Miss Ryan won the women's doubles with Helen Wills, and the mixed with the Australian, J. H. Crawford. Miss Ryan won the women's doubles at Wimbledon twelve times—twenty years separating her first win in 1914 and her last in 1934. I don't fancy that particular record will ever be beaten.

The year 1930 is also memorable in British lawn tennis history in that Miss Betty Nuthall won the American singles championship at Forest Hills—the only British woman ever to accomplish this achievement(17).

In 1931 came the first walk-over in the men's singles since the challenge round had been abolished, the American, Frank Shields, retiring to his compatriot, Sidney Wood. J. van Ryn won the men's doubles for the third year running, but this time with a new partner, G. M. Lott, who was a really magnificent doubles player. Lott won the men's doubles again at Wimbledon with another partner, and won the American men's doubles five times with three different partners. Cochet, who had been the top singles player in the world for three years, had gone out in the first round to that very steady and accurate British player, Nigel Sharpe. In the men's doubles, however, Cochet played brilliantly with Brugnon, and they came very near to victory.

Helen Wills, now Mrs. Wills-Moody, did not come over in 1931, and for the first and only time in lawn tennis history, two German girls fought out the final of the championship. Fräulein Cilly Aussem beat Fräulein Krahwinkel in two sets. Hers is the only German name on the singles roll of honour at Wimbledon.

An unseeded British pair, Mrs. Shepherd-Barron and Miss Phyllis Mudford (afterwards Mrs. M. R. King) won the ladies' doubles, just defeating in the final a most popular Franco-Belgian pair in Mlles Sigart and Metaxa.

The 1932 Wimbledon men's singles was won by a young newcomer from America in the person of H. Ellsworth Vines (27). This tall twenty-one-year-old Californian had won his own American championship the previous year. Cochet, once again seeded Number 1, and still regarded as the leading player in the world, went out in the second round to that very good British doubles player, I. G. Collins. Cochet immediately entered for the All-England Plate, a consolation prize for players defeated in the first two rounds and won it with considerable ease. This was the only time a player of such eminence has entered for this event, and Cochet's action not only increased the status of the Plate but showed what a great sportsman Cochet was.

Britain, whose star was now very much in the ascendant, had two players in the last eight. Perry was just beaten by the Australian, J. H. Crawford (29), but Austin beat Frank Shields (U.S.A.), the runner-up in the previous year, and then routed the Japanese champion, J. Satoh, who had beaten the holder, Sidney Wood. In the other semi-final Vines had slaughtered Crawford for the loss of only six games in the space of little over half an hour.

Austin was usually at his best against the hard-hitting American type of player, but he failed to take his chances in the final against Vines, who opened shakily; he was then swept off the court by a tornado of fierce and accurate hitting, the like of which I have never seen before or since. The last set, which Vines won to love, took less than ten minutes to play, and Austin said afterwards that he never saw some of his opponent's services let alone got a racket to them. Vines used very little spin on any of his strokes, thereby gaining in speed but losing in control. When his eye was really in, however, his power on all his strokes was crushing and his accuracy phenomenal.

Fräulein Aussem did not defend her women's title, and the return of Mrs. Helen Wills-Moody made the result a foregone conclusion.

Everyone was delighted to see Mlles Sigart and Metaxa, runners-up of the previous year, this time prove successful in the ladies' doubles. They were indeed a most colourful and sporting pair.

By 1933 Britain was really coming right to the fore in the world of lawn tennis. The hard-hitting, courageous left-hander, Miss Peggy Scriven, won the French championship— a victory which she repeated the following year; F. J. Perry won the first of his three American titles; Miss Betty Nuthall and Miss Freda James won the American doubles; and Britain won the coveted Davis Cup for the first time for twenty-one years. Yet the Wimbledon titles still eluded our players, and we failed to win one in 1933.

Crawford and Vines came through to the final of the men's singles, which on their previous year's encounter was expected to result in a comfortable win for Vines. But Crawford had improved a lot and at the "chess-board" type of game he had no superior. Once an opponent allowed Crawford to impose the rhythm and extreme accuracy of his game upon him he was lost, and eventually the more brilliant attack of Vines faltered in face of Crawford's impenetrable defence. Then, with his opponent exhausted, Crawford went to the net to deliver the *coup de grâce*. Few finer matches have ever been seen at Wimbledon between two such particularly sporting and popular antagonists.

Vines never played at Wimbledon again as he decided to turn professional and make a world tour with Tilden. Later he gave up tennis altogether in favour of golf, at which game he became an outstanding performer.

The highlight of the women's singles in 1933 was the great performance put up by the British girl, Miss Dorothy Round(16), in the final against the all-conquering Helen Wills-Moody, who won eventually in an atmosphere of tense excitement by 6–4, 6–8, 6–3. The gulf between the champion and her rivals had narrowed considerably but had not yet been bridged. Borotra and Brugnon retained their men's doubles title and Miss Ryan scored her eleventh success in the ladies' doubles—this time in partnership with the French player, Mme Simone Mathieu.

Nineteen thirty-four was an epoch-making Wimbledon for Britain. After a quarter of a century both the singles championships were won by British players. The last British win in the men's singles had been achieved by A. W. Gore in 1909. It was in that year that F. J. Perry, the 1934 winner, was born(25). He was the only child of a Labour Member of Parliament and was educated at Ealing County School. Perry was a natural athlete and ball-games player. Blessed with height, reach and superb physique, he was a life-long teetotaller and as fit a player as has ever stepped on to a court. He first became known as a table-tennis player, at which game he attained world honours. Then, as a member of the Herga Lawn Tennis Club at Harrow, and later of the Chiswick Park Lawn Tennis Club, he developed into a first-class tennis player.

Perry was really an entirely self-taught player—or rather an entirely natural player—for I have seldom met a champion who had so little idea of how he made his own strokes. His grip was quite peculiar and was unchanged for all his strokes. In fact he gripped his tennis racket as he did his table-tennis bat with an exaggerated continental grip which demanded a wrist of iron for stroking on the forehand wing. His forehand drive, taken early and hit extremely hard, was his best stroke. His backhand was a reliable, but not formidable, undercut stroke of the Crawford variety. His game was all attack. He had few strokes and did not go in for any frills in the way of drop shots and stop volleys, but the strokes which he had were always at his complete command. Perhaps his greatest assets were his perfect physical fitness, his extreme mobility, his mental and physical toughness, and, most of all, his supreme confidence in himself—which sometimes let him down by making him under-estimate his opponent. Just as the famous French team of the "Four Musketeers" had been built around the personality of Jean Borotra, so the revival of British lawn tennis was founded and developed around Fred Perry. Perry won the Wimbledon singles three years running, being the only man to do so since the challenge round had been abolished. Between 1931 and 1936 Perry played thirty-three Davis Cup singles for Britain, losing only three. He won the Australian singles in 1934, the American singles in 1933, 1934 and 1936 and the French singles in 1935. Although he was not quite in the same class as a doubles player, he won the Wimbledon doubles in 1932 with G. P. Hughes, a really fine exponent of the doubles game, and with the same partner won the Australian doubles in 1934, the French doubles in 1933 and several big Davis Cup encounters. After the 1936 Wimbledon he turned professional and defeated Vines in his professional début in New York and later at Wembley.

Perry always reminded me of the famous New Zealander, Tony Wilding, in the simplicity but cumulative power of his game and in his perfect physical condition. But Perry's manner was much more aggressive and flamboyant than Wilding's. He put British lawn tennis right back on the world map and kept it there for four years, with the assistance of those fine players—H. W. Austin, G. P. Hughes and C. R. D. Tuckey.

In most ways 1934 was a peak year for Wimbledon. The weather was good, the attendances were greater than ever and the King and Queen attended on several occasions. Only one thing rather spoilt the meeting, and that was a mysterious sickness, called by the newspapers "Wimbledon throat", which attacked some of the players and even forced one or two to retire from the tournament. Jack Crawford, the holder, was particularly badly affected by this curious afflic-tion, nevertheless he managed to reach the final after a tremendous five-set match against the American, Frank Shields. Perry reached the final after an equally tough five-setter against Sidney Wood, the American winner of 1931. Perry had the advantage of several previous victories over Crawford and knew how vitally important it was to hustle the Australian out of the leisurely, meticulously accurate type of game at which he was a past master. From 1–3 down in the first set Perry won twelve games running and ran out eventually a very worthy winner 6–3, 6–0, 7–5.

Miss Dorothy Round(16), from Dudley in the Midlands, gave further cause for jubilation to British supporters by winning the women's singles, in the absence of Mrs. Wills-Moody. After hard matches against the British player, Mrs. M. R. King, and the formidable French player, Mme Mathieu, Miss Round reached the final, where she defeated Miss Helen Jacobs in an exciting three-set match. Never has there been such excitement and enthusiasm in the Centre Court as when the two British winners, Perry and Miss Round, were presented to the King and Queen in the Royal Box after Miss Round's victory.

Miss Round was a lovely player to watch, with long sweeping classical strokes. She had a great deal of quiet strength of character, kept herself in perfect physical condition and was almost as sphinx-like on court as Helen Wills-Moody herself.

Borotra and Brugnon, who had held the men's doubles for two years, again reached the final, but failed to give away something like twenty years in age to the Americans, G. M. Lott and Lester Stoefen.

The powerful combination of Miss Ryan and Mme Mathieu won the women's doubles for the second year running. This was Miss Ryan's twelfth victory in this event and her last championship win at Wimbledon.

The 1935 Wimbledon was eventful for F. J. Perry's second successive victory in the men's singles. He thus became the first man to win the event two years running since the challenge round had been abolished. This time Perry's opponent in the final was the German, G. von Cramm(25). Perry had won the French and American singles championships since the previous Wimbledon, and was full of

27   H. Ellsworth Vines (U.S.A.),
Wimbledon champion, 1932

28   J. D. Budge (U.S.A.),
ranked Number 1 in the
world in 1937

29   The popular Australian, J. H.
Crawford, Wimbledon champion
of 1933

30 Geoff Brown, runner-up at Wimbledon in 1946

31 John Bromwich, runner-up at Wimbledon in 1948 and one of the greatest doubles players in the history of the game

confidence. Now aged twenty-six he had probably reached the peak of his game.

Mrs. Wills-Moody was over again but was reported to be short of match practice. She came early to play in the St. Georges Hill and Beckenham tournaments. In the former she lost a set to Miss Mary Hardwick, and in the latter was actually defeated most crushingly by the hard-hitting young left-handed British player, Miss Kay Stammers. Despite the fact therefore that she had won Wimbledon six times and indeed had only lost one match there—on her first visit in 1924, when she was only nineteen—she was only seeded fourth behind the holder, Miss Round, Frau Sperling and Miss Helen Jacobs (15). Miss Round was defeated in the semi-final by Miss Hartigan, possibly the soundest woman singles player Australia ever sent to Wimbledon. But the latter proved no match for Mrs. Will-Moody. "The other Helen" also came through to the final with a most impressive victory over Frau Sperling for the loss of only three games.

The battle of the Helens was certain to be dramatic by reason of the fact that they were not only great rivals on the court but were far from being friends. They both learnt their tennis in Berkeley, California, from the same coach, and, though they were both obviously going to be exceptionally good players, Helen Wills was always just a little better than Helen Jacobs—who came to be known as "the other Helen". And so a deep antagonism gradually arose between them. Both were beautiful to look upon; Helen Wills's expressionless face giving the impression of inner repose, whilst Helen Jacobs's more commanding Grecian profile seemed to imply the existence of hidden fires and unresolved complexities of character. Somehow these characteristics of the two Helens showed themselves in their strokes—or perhaps their strokes showed themselves in their characters. There was one fundamental weakness in Helen Jacobs's game; she lacked a steady topspin or flat-hit forehand drive which in general is the bedrock of a woman's game. This stroke never really came naturally to her, although she was always striving to cultivate it. Against most players her sliced forehand and backhand ground strokes were devastating weapons, but they could never quite stand up to the steady pounding of Helen Wills's deep hard-hit topspin drives. Often it seemed that Miss Jacobs had at last got the forehand stroke she wanted, but, alas, in times of stress it would always desert her. And it always seemed to me that it was this one weakness and uncertainty which just took the edge off the game of "the other Helen" and made her unhappy with herself.

Helen Wills had the perfectly rounded woman's game founded on baseline security and power, coupled with the ability to put away a volley and smash when necessary, which over a period of years is more likely to bring a woman a constant succession of victories than any other type of game.

Both Helens were strongly and athletically built—Helen Jacobs being almost masculine in her strength of limb, whilst Helen Wills was essentially feminine. Both had immense courage and resource. Both were great players.

The two Helens had met in many finals all over the world—two of them being at Wimbledon. But always Helen Wills had won and on only one occasion had she conceded a set to her rival.

And so the stage was set for a dramatic encounter, but no one imagined quite how dramatic it was going to be.

Mrs. Wills-Moody started playing perfect tennis and was soon leading 4–0. But Miss Jacobs was also playing wonderfully and drew up to 3–4, only to see her rival raise her game again to take the first set at 6–3. Then Miss Jacobs staged a resolute counter-attack to take the second set by the same score and square the match. The excitement was intense as the final set opened and the strain on both players was beginning to tell. Throwing in all her reserves of heart and nerve and sinew, Miss Jacobs attacked fiercely and went to 5–2. Then Mrs. Wills-Moody won a game. In the next game Miss Jacobs reached match point, but Mrs. Wills-Moody showed her greatness by remaining staunch and unmoved. She surmounted the crisis and drew up to 5–5, and then led 6–5. Miss Jacobs served two aces in the next game but the remorseless rhythm of Mrs. Wills-Moody's game and her devastating concentration took her out to victory at 7–5 in as gallant and exciting an encounter as has ever been seen at Wimbledon.

Crawford and Quist won the men's doubles for Australia, beating in the final the old American combination of Allison and van Ryn in as thrilling a contest as anyone could possibly wish to see. On his form that day Quist was quite superlative and established himself as one of the really great doubles players in the history of the game.

A British pair, Miss Kay Stammers and Miss Freda James, won the women's doubles, and another British pair in Dorothy Round and Fred Perry won the mixed doubles.

These were great days for Britain, and 1936 was to be greater still as four out of the five events went to home players. Perry and Miss Round won the mixed doubles for the second year running, this being Miss Round's third successive victory, and Kay Stammers and Miss James retained their women's doubles title. Perry had met with a bad accident in the previous year playing in the American Championships and was doubtful of his singles form. But he gained strength and confidence with every match and in the final had a virtual walk-over against von Cramm, who pulled a muscle in the second game.

After winning both his singles matches against Australia, to give Britain victory in the challenge round of the Davis Cup for the fourth year running, Perry departed to the professional ranks—a great champion indeed.

Two British pairs reached the final of the men's doubles, Hughes and Tuckey beating F. H. D. Wilde and C. E. Hare in five strenuous sets.

Miss Helen Jacobs, in the absence of Helen Wills-Moody, at last attained her heart's desire by winning the women's singles after being runner-up four times, but only after a very close call against the indomitable and indefatigable Frau Sperling.

This year was the last in which Mr. F. R. Burrow refereed the championships. He was then in his seventieth year and during his eighteen championships he had been responsible for putting well over eight thousand matches into court. He was succeeded by Mr. Hamilton Price.

Nineteen thirty-seven was Coronation Year, and it produced a really great young singles champion in Donald Budge of the U.S.A.(28). He was already ranked amongst the three top players in the world and had only narrowly been beaten by Perry in 1936, when only twenty years old. By 1937 Budge had still further strengthened his strong, aggressive game which had no weak point but included an attacking top-spin backhand drive which was just about as good a stroke on that wing as has ever been seen. In the semi-final von Cramm beat H. W. Austin of Great Britain, and then went down to the all-conquering Budge in three straight sets. This was the third successive year von Cramm had been runner-up, but, as usual, he took his defeat with perfect sportsmanship.

Miss Dorothy Round regained the women's singles championship, beating the holder, Miss Helen Jacobs, 6–4, 6–2, and then just managing to overcome the popular hard-hitting Polish champion, Panna Jedzrejowska, in the final. The latter just went down to Senorita Lizana at Forest Hills, U.S.A., in the final of the American championship.

Budge won the mixed with his compatriot, Miss Alice Marble, and the men's doubles with C. G. Mako, thus becoming a triple champion.

In the 1938 Wimbledon "Bunny" Austin reached the final of the singles for the second time, but was overwhelmed by Donald Budge, who now, at twenty-two, was a more complete player than ever and was the acknowledged leading player in the world. For the second year running he won the triple crown at Wimbledon and in this year he became the only player ever to win the four major championships of the world—Wimbledon, Forest Hills, U.S.A., Australian and French, all in the same year. Like Perry, Budge was a player of few strokes, but those he had were very very good. From the first stroke he sought to impose his attacking game on his adversary and to finish the rally with a winning volley at the earliest possible moment. Nineteen thirty-eight was the peak year of his game, and in the form he showed then he must be classed amongst the immortals.

Mrs. Wills-Moody was back again at Wimbledon for the last time, to notch her eighth singles championship and so set up an all-time record. After a long and very close struggle with Frau Sperling, she beat her old rival Helen Jacobs in the final for the loss of only four games—Miss Jacobs injuring her leg and only being able to limp about the court.

And so we come to 1939 and the last Wimbledon before the outbreak of the Second World War. Budge had departed to the professional ranks and his place was taken as Wimbledon champion by twenty-one-year-old Bobby Riggs (U.S.A.), who appeared at Wimbledon for the first time. Riggs was largely a baseline player at this time with wonderful ball control and a self-confidence even exceeding that of Perry. He only played at this one Wimbledon, winning all three events. After twice winning the American Championships he joined the professional ranks, later becoming professional champion for some years. Thus three successive Wimbledon champions—Perry, Budge and Riggs—had turned professional.

In the ladies' singles Miss Kay Stammers(50) of Great Britain had a fine win over Miss Helen Jacobs for the loss of only four games, but was then beaten all ends up in the final by Miss Alice Marble. Miss Marble had already won the American singles title twice and was to win it twice more before she turned professional. This year at Wimbledon she was in superb form, gaining the triple crown, as only Mlle Lenglen had done before her, by winning the women's doubles with Mrs. Fabyan and the mixed doubles with Riggs.

Miss Marble set a new style in women's tennis which was followed after the war by those other great champions, Margaret Osborne (Mrs. du Pont) and Miss Louise Brough. It was the power game in miniature of the modern male— big serve and constant net attack. I do not think it would have beaten the best game of Mlle Lenglen, nor Helen Wills-Moody, and in the 1938 Wightman Cup match the accurate forehand driving of Miss Kay Stammers had pierced Miss Marble's armour. But against most women this powerful net attack was devastating. Miss Marble was a pupil of the famous American coach, Miss "Teach" Tennant, afterwards to coach another famous American champion, Maureen Connolly. Alice Marble had had to fight ill-health and disappointment to reach the top, and would undoubtedly have won several more Wimbledons had it not been for the war. We can only judge her by her play at Wimbledon in 1939, and by that standard she was undoubtedly not only the outstandingly best woman player in the world, but one of the greatest women players ever.

With the coming of war a definite epoch in the history of

the game came to an end. Lawn tennis had become the most popular and universally played game in the world. Every year more tournaments were started and more clubs opened. In Britain the game was played in the Services and even in some of the public schools. Wimbledon still remained the acknowledged centre of the game though the leading lawn tennis nations were developing their own championships as the ubiquitous aeroplane continued to make the world smaller.

Everywhere more people were flocking to see the world's best players in action, and even the new Wimbledon had become too small to hold half the would-be spectators.

The lights went out in Europe and the blackout came to Britain, and in those areas for six weary and dangerous years the game of lawn tennis was virtually at a standstill.

For the period 1919 to 1939 these are my leading world players:

MEN'S SINGLES

1. W. T. Tilden	U.S.A.	7. J. Borotra France
2. R. Lacoste	France	8. J. H. Crawford Australia
3. H. E. Vines	U.S.A.	9. J. D. Budge U.S.A.
4. H. Cochet	France	10. R. J. Riggs U.S.A.
5. W. M. Johnston	U.S.A.	
6. F. J. Perry	Great Britain	

LADIES' SINGLES

1. Mlle Lenglen	France	7. Miss Betty Nuthall Great Britain
2. Mrs. Wills-Moody	U.S.A.	
3. Miss Alice Marble	U.S.A.	8. Miss Helen Jacobs U.S.A.
4. Mrs. L. A. Godfree	Great Britain	9. Miss Kay Stammers Great Britain
5. Miss Dorothy Round	Great Britain	10. Frau Sperling Germany
6. Fräulein C. Aussem	Germany	

MEN'S DOUBLES

1. W. L. Allison and J. van Ryn	U.S.A.
2. A. K. Quist and J. E. Bromwich	Australia
3. G. M. Lott and J. H. Doeg	U.S.A.

4. J. Borotra and J. Brugnon	France
5. W. T. Tilden and Vincent Richards	U.S.A.
6. H. Cochet and J. Brugnon	France
7. J. D. Budge and C. G. Mako	U.S.A.
8. R. Lycett and J. O. Anderson	Great Britain and Australia
9. R. V. Thomas and P. O'Hara Wood	Australia
10. W. T. Tilden and W. M. Johnston	U.S.A.

WOMEN'S DOUBLES

1. Mlle Lenglen and Miss Ryan	
2. Miss Marble and Miss Palfrey	U.S.A.
3. Miss Jacobs and Miss Palfrey	U.S.A.
4. Miss Ryan and Mme Mathieu	
5. Mrs. Watson and Mrs. Michell	Great Britain
6. Miss Nuthall and Mrs. Whittingstall	Great Britain
7. Miss K. Stammers and Miss James	
8. Mrs. Wightman and Miss Wills	U.S.A.
9. Mrs. Covell and Miss K. McKane	Great Britain
10. Mme Mathieu and Miss Yorke	
11. Mrs. Shepherd-Barron and Miss Mudford	Great Britain

Chapter Four

THE POST-WAR LAWN
TENNIS SCENE

JUST BEFORE THE WAR ended I paid a visit to the All-England Club and sat alone by the Centre Court. It was a place of ghosts. The sagging, derelict bomb damage gave it a bedraggled appearance which actually hid a spirit on the part of the war-time staff which was never extinguished even under the most depressing circumstances. But it was certainly almost impossible to imagine then that, within a year, the first post-war championship would be in progress.

But so it was, and within a year of the war ending the eagles had started to gather together. Mr. Hamilton Price, the pre-war referee, was dead, as was Mr. Dudley Larcombe, the secretary of the All-England Club. His assistant secretary, Miss Norah Cleather, had been carrying on most nobly during the war, and was actually living in the Club when the worst of the bombs fell.

The new secretary was Lieut.-Colonel Duncan Macaulay, who had been assistant referee to Mr. Hamilton Price, and it was on his very capable shoulders that the bulk of the work of getting things started again fell. With his charming and hard-working assistant secretary, Miss Bompas, he formed a team of loyal and devoted workers who started to get Wimbledon back on its feet again. To them the world of lawn tennis owes a great deal.

The new Wimbledon referee was Captain Trower, a badly disabled ex-serviceman of the First World War, who had made a considerable reputation as a referee of Club tournaments.

32 Miss Pauline Betz, the 1946 Wimbledon champion

33 (*Below*) Mrs. Pat Todd

34 Two great Americans. Miss Louise Brough (*right*) beats her friend
and doubles partner, Mrs. du Pont, in 1950 to take her third successive
Wimbledon title

What was the form with regard to the first post-war championships? Clearly Britain was out of the picture as she had suffered a more complete lawn tennis eclipse, from bombing and war conditions, than any other country. Her leading woman player, Mrs. Menzies (formerly Miss Kay Stammers), who had been runner-up to Miss Alice Marble in the last Wimbledon before the war, and had been ranked Number 2 in the world in 1939, was now a mother with family responsibilities and had virtually been out of tennis altogether for six years.

Miss Jean Nicoll, the junior champion of 1938, had become Mrs. Bostock. She had also suffered a gap of six years in her first-class lawn tennis career.

On the men's side, Tony Mottram, who had just begun to come into the international picture in 1939, was now twenty-six. He had distinguished himself as a bomber pilot during the war—but that had hardly advanced his tennis, and, though he was still destined to put up some fine performances for Britain, he never quite managed to bridge the gap the war years had wrought in his lawn tennis career.

The continent of Europe appeared to be in almost as bad a case as Britain. The famous "Four Musketeers" were heavy with (lawn tennis) years, though France had some fine players in their 1938 doubles champions, B. Destremau and Y. Petra, and in M. Bernard and P. Pellizza. Curiously enough, despite all the tremendous advantages held by the New World, it was France who provided the first post-war Wimbledon champion.

The Australian doubles champions of the immediate pre-war years, A. K. Quist and J. E. Bromwich, were now thirty-three and twenty-eight respectively—both in the veteran stage as international lawn tennis players go.

Least upset by the war of all the lawn tennis playing nations, it seemed certain that the United States would take the lead when the post-war championships started. It was not that the young American lawn tennis playing males were not called up for service in the armed forces: we know they were and what valiant service they performed. But whereas lawn tennis in Britain and on the Continent closed down completely during the war and only started up again with many creaks and groans, with ruined courts and grave shortages of equipment, the American lawn tennis courts and clubs remained in being, and the American championships continued all through the war. But it was in the sphere of women's tennis that the United States gained such a tremendous supremacy during the war years. Their young hopefuls of 1939 played and practised intensively during these years, and when international lawn tennis started again they swept the field.

The Wimbledon champion of 1939, R. L. Riggs, won the American championship of that year, lost it in 1940 to W. D. McNeill, won it again in 1941, and next appeared as a professional when he won that championship in 1946, 1947 and 1949. During the war years F. R. Schroeder won the American championship in 1942, J. R. Hunt in 1943 and F. A. Parker in 1944 and 1945. J. A. Kramer, G. Mulloy, W. F. Talbert and R. Falkenburg all appeared on the doubles championship roll during the war years and became names to conjure with after the war.

On the women's side Miss Alice Marble was American singles champion in 1939 and 1940, Mrs. E. T. Cooke (formerly Mrs. Palfrey-Fabyan) in 1941 and 1945, and Miss Pauline Betz in 1942-44.

From 1937 to 1940 Mrs. Fabyan and Miss Marble were doubles champions; then the former won with Miss Osborne in 1941, and from 1942, right away up to 1950 without a break, that great partnership of Miss Margaret Osborne (Mrs. du Pont) and Miss Louise Brough were doubles champions of the United States.

When the war started American women were leading the world. They could therefore retire to their own continent without fearing any deterioration from lack of first-class competition. They were indeed sufficient unto themselves, and during the war years they built up such strength in women's tennis that it was no wonder that the rest of the world could not compete when the war ended.

The favourite for the men's singles at the 1946 Wimbledon was Jack Kramer of the United States(40). He was then twenty-five, and six years earlier had been a doubles champion of the United States with his favourite partner, Ted Schroeder. Had it not been for his war service he would have undoubtedly won earlier singles championships both at Wimbledon and Forest Hills. He had actually attained Davis Cup honours before the war started. Kramer was certainly a great player without a weakness anywhere in his smooth, powerful, all-court game. He had height, reach, a tough physique and every shot in the game. Moreover, he was a fine match player and a great sportsman. But before the Wimbledon championships started he had developed a blister on his playing hand, and in the fourth round he went out in a terrific match to the burly, bespectacled Czech, Jaroslav Drobny. In the fifth round Dinny Pails of Australia lost to the gigantic Yvon Petra of France, and Drobny wilted before the tremendous double-handed hitting of Geoff Brown(30), the dark horse from Australia. Brown lost in a tremendous five-set final to Petra because he played for safety in the first two sets, which he lost, and then had too much ground to make up. Petra, a veteran of thirty, was certainly a surprising, and somewhat lucky, winner of the first post-war Wimbledon.

The ladies' singles was obviously going to be an all-American affair. Their two leading players, Miss Pauline Betz and Miss Margaret Osborne, had the week previously at Queen's Club fought out a really great singles final, just won by the safer ground strokes and slightly superior mobility of Miss Betz(32). They were supported by Miss Louise Brough, Miss Dodo Bundy and Miss Doris Hart—all capable of beating any woman in the world. Miss Betz did not look like losing a set on her way to the final, beating our young British hopeful, Miss Joy Gannon, for the loss of only one game in her second match. There were some desperate encounters in the other half of the draw. Miss Brough had the very greatest difficulty in beating her tenacious compatriot, Mrs. Pat Todd(33), and Miss Osborne only just defeated that lovely stylist, Doris Hart(37). In the semi-final Miss Brough beat her doubles partner, Miss Osborne, in two very close sets, but could then only take six games from Miss Betz in the final. This match provided a great contrast in styles. On the one hand the "big game" of Miss Brough, fierce service, great smash, and devastating volley; on the other, the more secure, more accurate, more baseline game of Miss Betz. Other things being equal, where women are concerned, it is the game of Miss Betz which generally triumphs because the attacking volleyer has not quite the mobility and stamina to bridge constantly that dangerous no-man's (and still more no-woman's) land between the service line and the net.

Miss Betz was an intelligent player and no mere automaton. She was a lovely mover about the court, and a great fighter in a tight match. Like Mrs. Bostock and Fred Perry of Britain she was also a table-tennis champion. Having won the American singles championship three times running during the war years, she had her greatest triumph in 1946 when she won at Wimbledon and Forest Hills and then turned professional. Had she not done so she would have had every chance of remaining on top of the world for two or three more years as she seemed to be just able to beat the other leading Americans on the big occasion.

Kramer showed that he was as good in doubles as singles by winning the doubles event with his compatriot, Tom Brown.

In the women's doubles, our two best British players, Mrs. Menzies and Mrs. Bostock, playing in partnership, reached the semi-final and then just went out to Miss Betz and Miss Hart, who, in the final, took the middle set from the American doubles champions of the previous four years, Miss Osborne and Miss Brough. This latter pair were very very hard to beat; they were both natural doubles players with powerful services, overhand and volley; they had the killer instinct of the boxing champion—essential for any great doubles pair; and they were close friends and perfect partners on and off the court. Their record in doubles was second to none in the whole history of the game and they were, in my opinion, one of the two best women's doubles pairs of all time. They were now successful at Wimbledon for the first time, and Miss Brough won the first of her mixed doubles championships with Tom Brown. Together, Miss Brough and Miss Osborne (afterwards Mrs. du Pont), were to win the women's doubles three years running (34), from 1948 to 1950, and Miss Brough was to win the mixed doubles twice more. In America they were to win the women's doubles together four more times, making a record of eight times in all—and one or other of them won the American mixed doubles every year from 1942 to 1950. In addition they won the French doubles three times. A marvellous record indeed! Certainly the feature of the first post-war Wimbledon was the superlative play of the American women.

It was a great effort on the part of the management—for which chief credit is due to Colonel Macaulay and his staff —that the Wimbledon championships could be opened again so soon after the war ended—and with such outstanding success. There was an acute shortage of every sort of lawn tennis equipment and such a shortage of labour and materials in Britain that the bomb damage on the Centre Court had to remain unrepaired. But the perfect Wimbledon courts, the envy of the whole lawn tennis world, were ready in time, as green and true and even more perfect than ever.

Miss Osborne won the 1946 French championship, having her revenge on Miss Betz. Jack Kramer won the men's singles at Forest Hills, and the fine American combination of G. Mulloy and W. F. Talbert won the men's doubles for the third time. In Melbourne, Australia, the two-man American team of F. R. Schroeder and J. A. Kramer won back the Davis Cup which the United States had lost to Australia at Philadelphia in 1939. In the Australian championships John Bromwich registered his second singles win, his first being in 1939; and Mrs. Nancye Bolton won the women's singles. The veterans, A. K. Quist and John Bromwich, won the men's doubles for the fourth time running—their last win being six years earlier in 1940.

World lawn tennis was back in its stride again with a vengeance—with America supreme.

The first major event in the 1947 season as far as Great Britain was concerned was the Hard Court Championship at Bournemouth, which, in this year, re-assumed its international aspect—with the result that every title went overseas. South Africa's leading male player, Eric Sturgess, who was to go so near to winning several of the major national titles in the following years, was the winner of three events. He won the singles fairly comfortably and the men's doubles and mixed with E. Fannin and Mrs. Sheila Summers, who were also members of the popular South African visiting team.

The South African woman champion, Mrs. Mary Muller, the fourth member of the team, never quite touched her South African form during her visit to Britain.

Mrs. Nancye Bolton, the hard-hitting Australian champion, took forty minutes to beat Miss Joan Curry in the women's singles final. There have been few more lovely hitters of a tennis ball than Mrs. Bolton, and no more popular or more sporting champion. But her complete scorn for safety-first tactics and the abandoned joy of her hitting made her too prone to errors to beat the leading Americans.

Britain supplied the finalists in the women's doubles in Mrs. Menzies and Miss Quertier, but they could not quite compete with the flashing strokes of Mrs. Bolton, backed by the cool experience of her compatriot, Mrs. Nell Hopman.

Jack Kramer was a natural and warm favourite for the 1947 Wimbledon, and, in the absence of Miss Betz, the three top-seeded Americans, Margaret Osborne, Louise Brough and Doris Hart, were in a class by themselves. As it turned out, Kramer, now at the very peak of his form, had a very easy victory. Two surprise results in the men's singles event were the victories of twenty-three-year-old Budge Patty of the United States over John Bromwich of Australia and Jaroslav Drobny. The final, in which Kramer beat his compatriot, Tom Brown, was really almost a walk-over.

Mrs. Sheila Summers, South Africa's leading player, overcame Mrs. Pat Todd, but was then hit off the court by the powerful game of Miss Margaret Osborne. Miss Doris Hart, now twenty-two and strengthening her game every year, managed to overcome Miss Brough, but had not the reserve of strength to repeat her victory against Miss Osborne.

But without any doubt the real thrill of the 1947 Wimbledon was the grand victory of Miss Hart and Mrs. Todd (33) over the world champions, Miss Osborne and Miss Brough. The latter led 5–3 and 40–love on Miss Brough's service in the final set, and it would have been a rash man indeed who would then have laid any odds at all on the victory of the under-dogs. It was Mrs. Todd's determination and brilliance which inspired her partner at this stage of the game to bring off one of the most dramatic victories in this event ever seen at Wimbledon.

The mixed doubles was won by the two-handed wizard, John Bromwich, of Australia, in partnership with Miss Louise Brough. They were certainly one of the strongest mixed doubles partnerships ever seen at Wimbledon. They won again the next year at Wimbledon, and won the 1947 mixed doubles at Forest Hills.

The gallant Mrs. Todd achieved even greater triumphs in the French championships where she beat both Miss Osborne and Miss Hart, to win the singles event; but in the women's doubles Miss Brough and Miss Osborne reversed the Wimbledon result by beating Miss Hart and Mrs. Todd in two straight sets.

These 1947 French championships were played in tremendous heat on the slow, airless hard courts of the Stade Roland Garros in Paris—in fact, so much did the heat affect both players and spectators that it was decided to revert to pre-war practice and play these championships in May—which was obviously a much more suitable time of year.

The American National Championships were divided, as usual, into two sections—the men's and ladies' doubles being played at the Longwood Cricket Club, Boston, in August, and the singles and mixed doubles at Forest Hills in September. The Wimbledon champion, Jack Kramer, retained his title against a very strong challenge from Frank Parker. Miss Brough won her first major national singles title, beating Mrs. Bolton in the semi-final and her doubles partner, Miss Osborne, in the final.

Once again the United States emerged as the top lawn tennis playing nation, though, with the transfer of Kramer to the professional ranks, the field was to become rather more level. Australia was just starting to strengthen her challenge, but both France and Britain were right out of the international picture.

An interesting event in the British lawn tennis season was the re-appearance of the famous Frenchman, Jean Borotra, in the International Club match played on wood at Queen's Club in October. Borotra, now nearing fifty and very much in the veteran stage, still showed distinct glimpses of his former greatness.

In May 1948, for the second year running, Eric Sturgess (43) of South Africa won the British Hard Court singles title at Bournemouth. An even stronger player than he had been the previous year in every department of his essentially sound, error-free game, he lost only twenty games in the twelve sets he had to play to reach the final, where he again defeated the veteran ex-Polish international, I. Tloczynski, this time for the loss of only eight games. And for the second year running Sturgess was the winner of three events. It was noticeable that he was now much more ready to go to the net in a single than he had been in previous years, with the result that he was winning his matches more quickly and with much less fatigue. It was only the lack of severity in any department of his game which kept him from the highest honours.

The women's events at Bournemouth were confined to home players. Miss Joan Curry, the previous year's runner-up, went out unexpectedly to the much improved Miss Georgie Woodgate, who then went down fighting to Mrs. Bocquet. Miss Joy Gannon, from whom much had been expected, failed to beat Mrs. Lines in the second round. In the bottom half of the draw Mrs. Betty Hilton came through comfortably to the semi-final losing only four games to Miss Jean Quertier.

In the semi-final Mrs. Hilton was somewhat lucky to beat that fine little stroke-maker, Miss Gem Hoahing, one of the most popular players in British tournaments. At set-all Miss Hoahing had Mrs. Hilton's dashing all-court game in tatters, and Mrs. Hilton near to exhaustion; but a rain storm came to her rescue and, when the match went into court again, Mrs. Hilton was in a winning position before Miss Hoahing, always a slow starter, had got going.

In the final Mrs. Bocquet appeared somewhat overawed by her opponent's reputation, and Mrs. Hilton had only to keep the ball in play to win as she pleased. In the doubles, the top-seeded pair, Mrs. Hilton and Mrs. Menzies, came through successfully, beating the younger combination of Miss Gannon and Miss Quertier in the final for the loss of only three games.

I note that when describing the play in the Queen's Club tournament before the Wimbledon championships I wrote: "The twenty-year-old Australian, Frank Sedgman, is the most promising player I have seen since Donald Budge, and I predict a Wimbledon crown for him in the not too distant future. He has everything in the way of strokes, excellent physique, a fine temperament and perfect court manners, and I don't believe that success will spoil him." My prediction was certainly to be borne out to the full.

In the absence of Jack Kramer the 1948 Wimbledon was a most open event. The seedings were made for a Parker-Bromwich final, but Lennart Bergelin, the fair-haired, young Swedish champion, beat Parker in the fourth round in a memorable five-set match, in which Parker showed a standard of sportsmanship which I have rarely seen surpassed. The tall, highly-strung, twenty-three-year-old American, Bob Falkenburg, who had been ranked seventh in the U.S.A. the year before and was seeded seventh at Wimbledon, carried altogether too many guns for the young Australian, Frank Sedgman. The men's singles between the twenty-nine-year-old Australian, John Bromwich, and Bob Falkenburg, was a poor match, and, until the very dramatic closing stages, it was almost dull: then it was harrowing and breath-taking in turn. Bromwich threw the match away, as he himself admitted, by the lack of speed in all his shots, and particularly by his failure to put the ball away either on the volley or overhead. When he appeared to have the match in his hands he played for safety and gave Falkenburg his chance to win the championship.

The British Number 1, Tony Mottram, much distinguished himself by beating Italy's leading singles player, G. Cucelli, in a tremendous five-set match—Cucelli having beaten the much favoured J. Drobny the round before. Mottram then went on to gain a place in the last eight by beating the Belgian champion, P. Washer, before going out to Gardnar Mulloy.

The champion, Bob Falkenburg, came in for a good deal of criticism on several occasions during the championship, and particularly in the final, by the unduly long "rests" he took on court between some of the points. He was also criticised for the somewhat ostentatious way in which he threw away a set in the final to allow himself time to recover his wind. However, it must be said that Falkenburg was a young man who had obviously very much outgrown his strength

and he just had not the physical capacity to play through a hard five-set match at top speed. However, the fact remained that he won—and won most gallantly when all the odds seemed to be against him.

In the men's doubles Australia started to demonstrate supremacy in this type of game—a supremacy which was to increase steadily during the next few years. Young Frank Sedgman and the veteran John Bromwich, one of the cleverest and best doubles players there has ever been, fitted in remarkably well and were popular winners of the event.

In the ladies' singles Britain had two players in the last eight—Mrs. Jean Bostock and Miss Jean Quertier, who eliminated the two top South African players—Mrs. Mary Muller and Mrs. Sheila Summers. But the rest of the story was all American. Miss Doris Hart played brilliantly to beat Mrs. du Pont in one semi-final, and Miss Brough beat Mrs. Todd in two straight sets in the other. For the second year running the somewhat frail Miss Hart just could not find the strength to beat the other "Queen of the court" at the end of a strenuous Wimbledon fortnight.

This year Britain produced a pair in the semi-final of the women's doubles in Mrs. Jean Bostock and Mrs. Molly Blair. This pair had much distinguished themselves a few weeks before by defeating the Wimbledon champions, Miss Doris Hart and Mrs. Pat Todd, in the Wightman Cup doubles, but they just failed to repeat the performance against the same pair in the semi-finals of the championships. Once again Miss Brough and Mrs. du Pont won the event. Thus Miss Brough joined Mlle Lenglen and Alice Marble as a winner of all three events at the same Wimbledon, and she had certainly established herself as the leading lady player of the year—although at Forest Hills she had to surrender her American title to Mrs. Margaret du Pont.

The British tennis season ended up with rather a momentous National Covered Courts Championship at Queen's Club. The amazing Jean Borotra in his fifty-first year won the singles title for the tenth time in his career. Geoffrey Paish, the British Davis Cup player, who opposed him in the final, had not been born when Borotra first played for France in the Davis Cup. In his hey-day Borotra's favourite surface had always been wood, and it was on the fast East court at Queen's that he had put up some of his greatest performances. At fifty even Borotra's magnificently fit body did not recover quickly from fatigue, and after a hard mixed doubles the night before he was a tired man when he went on court for his singles final. But he rationed out his physical resources just as cleverly as he always had done, making the rallies as short as he could and going for the vital games. In his early twenties there were many who said that his constant volleying attack would burn up his physical and nervous resources very early; but it was Borotra and Cochet, the confirmed attackers in the forecourt, who outlasted, in the championship class, by many years all their contemporaries, with the single exception of Tilden. Borotra kept himself fit by a most rigorous self-discipline and training, and his very active business life helped to keep him young and resilient in mind as well as body.

Miss Gem Hoahing beat Miss Joan Curry in the women's singles final, and Miss Curry and Miss Quertier won the women's doubles.

The veteran A. K. Quist won his third Australian singles championship—his first having been twelve years earlier in 1936. Once again he and Bromwich won the men's doubles and Mrs. Nancye Bolton won the women's singles.

I must make some mention here of the two-handed style of play of which a great deal more had been seen in post-war lawn tennis than ever before in the history of the game. When the young Australian, Vivian McGrath, appeared at Wimbledon in 1933, aged only seventeen, and smote the ball on his backhand, holding the racket in both hands, he was put down as a freak. The purists pointed out everything that was wrong with his involved style of play, and lawn tennis coaches the world over hoped that such a thing would not happen again. There were, indeed, obvious disadvantages to the two-handed method; yet Vivian McGrath became one of the best ten players in the world.

But with McGrath's passing from the top ranks of world lawn tennis another two-handed player appeared, also an Australian, and he scaled even dizzier heights than those reached by Vivian McGrath. John Bromwich, with his two-handed forehand, became ranked amongst the world's three foremost players before the war(31). And at the 1946 Wimbledon two other two-handed players made their appearance. Francesco Segura, champion of Ecuador, was ranked as high as Number 3 in the U.S.A. as an amateur, and later became the world's professional champion. Geoff Brown(30) of Australia reached three Wimbledon finals at his first appearance at the All-England Club. So the two-handed style could no longer be laughed off.

The four main protagonists of the two-handed method whom I have mentioned varied in the execution of their strokes, and between them demonstrated different variations of this peculiar style. Vivian McGrath was entirely normal in his method of play, save that on his backhand wing he gripped the racket with two hands. Segura stroked on both wings with two hands; and both Bromwich and Geoff Brown served and smashed right-handed, stroked on the backhand wing left-handed, and used both hands for drives and volleys on the forehand wing. Segura's method appeared to have one definite disadvantage as compared with that of Bromwich and Brown. His two-handed grip on both sides of his body did reduce his reach, as anyone can demonstrate to himself quite easily. It might be argued that from the point of view of reach alone a single-handed ambidexterous style would be best—such as was adopted by the Italian, G. de Stefani, and after the Second World War by the scintillating little American player, Miss Beverly Baker. But this style involves weaknesses in the middle section—particularly the fatal weakness of the change over of the racket from one hand to the other.

Both Bromwich and Brown served and smashed right-handed, drove and volleyed on the backhand side with their left hands, and drove and volleyed on the forehand side with both hands on the racket. The two-handed grip on the forehand certainly makes the player look a bit cramped and tucked up, but it does favour the taking of an early ball and facilitates extreme accuracy on drop shot and lob. From a position on the court just inside the service line Bromwich and Brown could punch a volley two-handed which the ordinary player would be content to block. Bromwich's style did involve a slight change of grip, but not nearly as much as people imagine, as his left hand hardly changed its place on the racket, except for service and smash—when, of course, it was removed altogether.

It was, however, in the service that the protagonists of the two-handed method came up against a real problem. What was to be done with the second ball if the first service was right? At one time Segura used to stuff it into his pocket—not a very satisfactory procedure. Brown used to throw his away—to which on certain occasions his opponents raised objections, as the procedure was certainly distracting to the eye. At one time Brown tried to adopt a new method of placing the second service ball by his right foot whilst he served the first—but that would have been very upsetting to the rhythm of the service for anyone who had a fast or severe delivery.

But it is noteworthy that with all the disadvantages in the curtailment of reach, etc., which must be involved by the two-handed method, these players who have taken it up have gone from strength to strength and reached the topmost rung of the ladder.

The opening of the 1949 lawn tennis season in Great Britain showed Mottram and Paish, her two stalwarts in the male line, and Miss Quertier and Mrs. Walker-Smith, the leading women players, to be in their best form; but it was the tenacious Joan Curry who won the Hard Court Championships at Bournemouth, beating Miss Tuckey, Miss Georgie Woodgate, Mrs. Jean Walker-Smith and finally Miss Jean Quertier in a series of needle matches. The final match produced a grand display of fighting tennis which did credit to both players. Miss Curry, who was also for several years the British squash rackets champion, was a fine athlete and match player at both games. On slow hard courts she was very hard to beat, and even on the fast grass turf of Wimbledon played some good matches for Britain against the leading Americans.

In the women's doubles an unseeded pair, Miss Gannon and Miss Rodgers, did exceedingly well to reach the final and fully extended the strong combination of Mrs. Hilton and Mrs. Halford.

The men's singles was won by P. Masip of Spain over the

old champion, Henri Cochet of France, now aged forty-seven. Eighteen years earlier Cochet had been the leading player in the world and, although giving away seventeen years to Masip, he very nearly carried the match to a fifth set.

The American, F. A. Parker, won the French Championships in May, and Mrs. du Pont (the former Miss Margaret Osborne) was the women's singles winner. The Americans, R. A. Gonzales and F. A. Parker, won the men's doubles, and the inevitable Miss Brough and Mrs. du Pont the women's.

Never before had there been such a demand for tickets at Wimbledon as there was in 1949. With the exception of William Talbert, Miss Doris Hart and Miss Beverly Baker, all of the U.S.A., every one of the world's top men and women had entered. The men's singles event was as open as it could be and of so high a class that players like Gardnar Mulloy and Budge Patty and Asboth of Hungary were unseeded. Writing on the subject the week before the championships I said: "I am inclined to fancy the chance of Ted Schroeder who is second to Gonzales in the American ranking and is competing at his first Wimbledon. . . . For the women's singles I think that this year I should have picked Miss Doris Hart had she been able to enter. There is little to choose between those other two great Americans, Miss Louise Brough and Mrs. Margaret du Pont, and I shall select the former, who has hardly yet reached her peak, to retain her championship."

In actual fact my two selections Schroeder and Miss Brough turned out to be correct. Mrs. du Pont was, however, American and French champion and was favoured by many to regain the Wimbledon championship.

Ted Schroeder (41), already twenty-eight, and nearing the veteran stage as lawn tennis players go, was a strong player and tough fighter in both singles and doubles. He had been Kramer's favourite partner. With his rolling gait on court, his sportsmanship and good humour he became an instant favourite with the Wimbledon crowd.

The seeded players in the men's singles were Schroeder, Gonzales, Parker and Falkenburg (the holder) of the U.S.A., John Bromwich of Australia and Eric Sturgess of South

Africa. No British players reached the third round. Mottram went out to his old enemy, Cucelli of Italy, and Paish succumbed in a long five-set match to V. Cernik of Czechoslovakia.

The first real sensation was when R. Gonzales (39) the young American champion, was beaten in the fourth round by that tough little giant-killer, Geoff Brown of Australia. Gonzales, a fine mover and stroke maker, was lulled into a sense of false security when he won the first set quite easily at 6–2. But in the next set Brown, who had so nearly beaten Petra in the 1946 final, then struck his best form. His left-handed passing shots, combined with his dynamic double-handed drives on his forehand wing, continually had Gonzales guessing. Brown had got his teeth into the match and refused to let go. Under his determined onslaught Gonzales crumpled and was well beaten in a runaway 6–1 fourth set. But Brown met his Waterloo in the next round against Jaroslav Drobny (42), the burly Czech breaking up his driving game with drop shots and lobs. Bromwich had his revenge on Falkenburg, his conqueror in the final of the year before, and Sturgess just managed to beat Parker in five sets. Talking to Sturgess in the dressing-room just before he went on court I had told him I felt he could win this match—if only he himself would feel he could. But Parker played so much the same type of game and had always played it just that little bit better. However, half-way through the match Sturgess really started to feel it could be done—and he did it in no uncertain fashion, with scores of 6–1, 6–3 in the last two sets of a tense, but not wildly exciting five-set match. So the semi-finalists were Drobny, Bromwich, Sturgess and Schroeder, who had had the narrowest squeak of his life against the splendid young Australian, Frank Sedgman. Sedgman only lost this match through inexperience after having had two match points.

In the semi-finals Drobny slaughtered Bromwich, being altogether too severe for the Australian wizard. It was rather a tragedy that Bromwich should have had a Wimbledon championship in his hands the year before—and literally thrown it away. The Fates rarely give one a second chance. Sturgess gave all he had against Schroeder, and when he led by two sets to one he appeared to have a chance. But you don't attain a Number 1 world ranking for nothing, and in a crisis, almost as unpleasant as the one he had experienced the round before against Sedgman, Schroeder trod on the gas and won the last two sets for the loss of only three games.

His men's final against Drobny turned out to be the least testing five-setter of the four he had to play. In fact it is difficult to explain how he allowed it to go to five sets— unless it was that, having taken his usual first set to settle down, he established such a complete ascendancy in the next two that he subconsciously let up. Unusually uncertain over-head, and as usual very vulnerable on his backhand wing, Drobny yet kept the match going by means of his great service and flashing forehand drive. These two strokes were two of the greatest ever possessed by one player in the whole history of the game. But whenever Schroeder needed a point it was almost his for the taking with a drive or service to Drobny's backhand which provoked the sliced soaring return and gave a great volleyer a certain kill at the net. So Schroeder came and saw and conquered at Wimbledon at his first attempt— and Wimbledon never saw him again. At twenty-eight he was undoubtedly past his best and he was not the complete player that Kramer was. But as a tactician and lion-hearted fighter, with seemingly inexhaustible physical reserves, I have never seen his superior on a tennis court.

There were some fine matches in the men's doubles. Britain's leading pair, Mottram and Paish, came through to the last eight and went down fighting to the strongly fancied Americans, Mulloy and Schroeder. The holders, Bromwich and Sedgman, went out to Budge Patty and Sturgess, who in turn succumbed in five sets to Gonzales and Parker. The latter pair beat Mulloy and Schroeder in the final with surprising ease.

And now to join the ladies. Britain had four players in the last eight of the singles—Mrs. Blair, Mrs. Walker-Smith, Mrs. Dawson-Scott and Mrs. Hilton. But that was as far as it went. Mrs. Walker-Smith battled stoutly against Mrs. Todd (U.S.A.) and took a set; Mrs. Dawson-Scott lost to Mrs. Helen Rihbany (U.S.A.) in two long vantage sets; and Mrs. Blair and Mrs. Hilton were unfortunate enough to meet Miss Brough and Mrs. du Pont respectively. Enough said! Miss Brough slaughtered Mrs. Todd for the loss of only three games, and Mrs. du Pont lost only four to Mrs. Rihbany.

The final lasted two hours. After leading 4–0 in the first set Miss Brough only managed to win it at 10–8. Mrs. du Pont's determined counter-attack gave her the second set at 6–1 in only twelve minutes play. The final set took nearly an hour and there was hardly a point in it either way until Miss Brough led at 8–7. Mrs. du Pont saved a match point and the umpire actually gave the match to Miss Brough in error. Then Mrs. du Pont saved another match point and squared at 8–all. But a gallant loser had shot her bolt, and Mrs. du Pont could do no more.

Such a needle match between great friends and doubles partners is rather difficult to assess at its true value. It was certainly fine tennis, and I believe that only Suzanne Lenglen, Helen Wills-Moody, Alice Marble and Pauline Betz could have defeated either of them at this time. But, knowing them both very well, I am in no doubt whatsoever that it was in no sense a staged "professional" exhibition. Both tried their best to win. Yet I must say it always bored me very much to see Louise Brough playing Margaret du Pont in a single. They knew one another's game too well. It wanted a second Doris Hart to add another challenge and, possibly, raise the game of the two "Queens" to even greater heights.

In the women's doubles Britain had four pairs in the last eight, the others being one from South Africa and three from the United States. The South African pair could make nothing of the champions, Miss Brough and Mrs. du Pont, who won as they pleased 6–2, 6–2. Miss Gannon and Mrs. Hilton beat their elders, and one time betters, the Hon. Mrs. B. F. Glover and Mrs. Gordon—the latter as Margot Lumb one of the greatest women squash players ever—for the loss of only four games. Miss Shirley Fry and Mrs. Rihbany (U.S.A.) just survived a terrific struggle against Mrs. Blair and Miss Quertier; and Mrs. Pat Todd, playing this year with a new and glamorous partner, Miss "Gussie" Moran(36), had no difficulty in disposing of Miss Patsy Rodgers and Mrs. Jean Walker-Smith—though the American pair had been extremely lucky to beat that excellent regular British doubles combination of Mrs. Dawson-Scott and Miss Wilford. In the semi-finals Miss Brough and Mrs. du Pont beat the last British pair, Miss Gannon and Mrs. Hilton, for the loss of only two games, and Mrs. Todd and Miss Moran lost only five in disposing of Miss Fry and Mrs. Rihbany.

The great trouble about British women's doubles after the Second World War was that the players just would not stick to one partner for more than half a season at a time. And here the British Lawn Tennis Association were greatly at fault for not asserting more direction and control. Doubles is essentially a team game, and many are the examples of a good pair beating opponents of much greater individual brilliance. It seemed as though Britain had cast aside all the old lessons of good doubles play and was content merely to watch the Americans demonstrating them. But, of course, the real trouble was that Britain just hadn't got the players after the war with a real natural aptitude for the doubles game. Two notable exceptions were Mrs. Kay Menzies and Mrs. Jean Bostock, who, despite the fact that neither possessed a "big" American service, could challenge comparison with the best in the world. But they didn't fit as a pair and wisely broke up their partnership. Also, of course, Mrs. Menzies was some years past her best when the post-war lawn tennis era started, and it is a remarkable tribute to her class and her physical fitness that she was able to keep her place so long in the top ranks. Mrs. Bostock did find a sympathetic partner in Mrs. Molly Blair, and they had just started to deliver a really stern challenge to the top American pairs when Mrs. Bostock retired from the game for family reasons. Miss Jean Quertier was a brilliant natural doubles player and the best British mixed player in the post-war years. She put up some fine performances with Geoffrey Paish, who understood her wonderfully well, but she was temperamentally difficult to partner—though she and Mrs. Menzies, had the latter been five years younger, might have formed a most formidable combination.

The women's doubles final was a very close affair indeed. Miss Brough and Mrs. du Pont were never happy about the outcome and were admittedly upset by the laughter and applause of the crowd over Miss Moran's much advertised glamour garments, which she was wearing for the first time on the Centre Court. I have said something on this subject in the first chapter of this book, and will not dilate on it here. But Miss Moran was really a fine player, and under better direction might well have astonished the world—for the quality of her tennis alone. In America—where the crowd would have whistled her off court, even if the management had ever allowed her to appear in some of her Wimbledon attires—I have seen her play some really fine tennis. But, although seeded in both singles and doubles at this Wimbledon, she never did herself justice and went out in the former to Miss Gem Hoahing, and in the doubles final she could never attain the concentration and unselfconsciousness to give her best support to that fine doubles player, Mrs. Pat Todd. Miss Brough and Mrs. du Pont heaved a sigh of relief when they nosed the match out at 8–6, 7–5 to win their third Wimbledon doubles.

The mixed doubles final between the holders, John Bromwich and Louise Brough, and the South Africans, Eric Sturgess and Sheila Summers, was as exciting a match as one could wish to see. Only as the shadows of evening were falling across the Centre Court and the clocks had struck eight o'clock did the gallant South Africans just pull it out in the final set.

But what a tremendous feat of physical and mental endurance had been performed by Miss Brough on the final day! After more than four and a half hours of actual play on the Centre Court, she only just failed to set up a Wimbledon record of becoming the first woman player in the history of the game to win the singles, doubles, and mixed doubles titles in successive years.

In the American Championships R. Gonzales retained his singles title after a two-and-a-half hour struggle against the Wimbledon champion, Ted Schroeder. The latter won the first set at 18–16, and Gonzales showed great match playing qualities in overcoming this exhausting setback and finally turning the tables on the most redoubtable match player in the world. But age is a tremendous factor in tennis of this class, and Gonzales was seven years the younger man.

Certainly I have seldom seen a faster or more thrilling encounter in America or anywhere else. Australia started to assert her ascendancy in the men's doubles game by winning the American title for the first time since the war with Bromwich and Sidwell. Miss Brough and Miss Osborne won the women's doubles for the eighth year running. In the women's singles Miss Hart scored a brilliant victory over Miss Brough, who was reacting from her Wimbledon triumphs, but once again failed to beat the second "Queen" in the final. Mrs. du Pont won 6–4, 6–1 in only forty minutes play. Mrs. Betty Hilton had much distinguished herself in the women's singles event by becoming the first semi-finalist Britain had produced at Forest Hills since Mary Hardwick (Mrs. Hare) in 1940. But Betty was quite outclassed in the semi-final by Mrs. du Pont.

In the British National Covered Court Lawn Tennis Championships, played at Queen's Club in October, Jean Borotra created a record which will probably stand for all time in winning his eleventh Covered Court Singles Championship at fifty-one years of age—a really stupendous athletic achievement. Miss Joan Curry, the British hard court champion, also became the covered court champion when she overwhelmed Miss Jean Quertier for the loss of only one game.

Frank Sedgman succeeded A. K. Quist as Australian singles champion, and Miss Doris Hart won the Australian women's singles title. Yet again the inevitable veterans, Quist and Bromwich, won the Australian men's doubles.

By 1949 the British lawn tennis tournament season had settled down into a more or less steady routine with almost every week booked for one tournament or another. Up to the beginning of May our British climate confines play to hard courts or wood. This period finishes with the British Hard Court Championships at Bournemouth in the last week of April. The grass court season is generally considered to open at Surbiton in the last week of May, and things then gradually boil up to Queen's Club, the "curtain-raiser for Wimbledon", in the third week of June. The Wimbledon Championships follow in the last week of June and first week of July. Then come the holiday tournaments, interrupted by

35 The outside courts at Wimbledon in 1948

37 Miss Doris Hart (U.S.A.), Wimbledon champion in 1951

36 Miss "Gussie" Moran (U.S.A.), in play on the Centre Court in 1949

the very serious Inter-County week at the end of July. Finally in September we get back to hard courts again. And the season ends with the Covered Court Championships at Queen's Club in October.

There is also a big programme of junior tournaments in August and September, finishing with the Junior Championships of Great Britain at Wimbledon.

But the ubiquitous aeroplane has made lawn tennis into an all-the-year round game, and by 1950 never a month went by without there being some national championship in some part of the world which was accessible by air to the world's leading players. Thus when we are getting ready for Christmas in Britain our leading players are setting forth to take part in the Calcutta Championships—and so it goes on throughout other parts of the world at different times of the year.

In the 1950 Championships of Australia Frank Sedgman retained his singles title, and Miss Brough won the women's singles. The amazing Australians, Quist and Bromwich, registered their eighth successive victory in the men's doubles event.

The 1950 British Hard Court title was won by J. Drobny, who also won the men's doubles with his Czech compatriot, V. Cernik. Miss Joan Curry retained her women's singles title, and Mrs. Hilton won the women's doubles for the third year running—each time with a different partner. This time it was Miss Kay Tuckey, and in the final they beat Miss Quertier and Mrs. Walker-Smith 4–6, 6–3, 6–2.

The French Championships in May had seen Budge Patty (U.S.A.) in fine form. He had won some great matches in previous years, but had never had the mental or physical stamina to achieve a national title against the world's leading players. This year he had really trained—and the French title was his just reward. Miss Doris Hart won the women's singles title, and also the women's doubles with her new partner, Miss Shirley Fry.

There was a magnificent entry for the Queen's Club tournament before the Wimbledon Championships. This tournament can never be taken as a direct guide to the chances of the champions, but it does give an opportunity for all the leading protagonists to cross swords with one another—and to sharpen their weapons if necessary.

Ted Schroeder, the men's singles holder, did not come to Wimbledon to defend his title, and Gonzales, the American champion, had joined the professional ranks the previous October. Frank Sedgman, the Australian title holder, who was seeded first, was suffering from a strained wrist, and I remarked in my pre-Wimbledon article in the *Sunday Times* that I had never known an unfit man to come successfully through the strenuous Wimbledon fortnight. W. Talbert (U.S.A.), the second seed, was ranked immediately after Gonzales and Schroeder in America. Though nearly thirty-two, and making his first appearance at Wimbledon, he was very highly fancied. I certainly thought myself that he had a great chance.

No British player survived to the last sixteen of the men's singles, and until that stage there were no surprises. Drobny beat McGregor of Australia with the greatest ease; hard-hitting Victor Seixas, ranked only Number 12 in America, was too severe for John Bromwich of Australia; and Budge Patty beat Billy Talbert in a match which was interrupted by rain. Sedgman beat Drobny in the semi-final, after losing the first two sets. Sedgman, who had played throughout with his wrist heavily bandaged and had taken part—I thought most ill-advisedly—in all events, was a very tired man by the final day, but Budge Patty, who for the first time had allied a thoroughly fit body to an agile mind and artistic stroke production, was a very worthy winner.

The men's doubles was won by that most remarkable Australian pair, John Bromwich and Adrian Quist. These two won the Australian doubles eight times running, despite the gap of five war years between their third and their fourth wins. Quist won at Wimbledon in 1935 with J. H. Crawford and put up a superlative performance. When he won this year with Bromwich he was thirty-seven years old. In 1948 Bromwich took young Frank Sedgman as his Wimbledon partner—and won. In 1949 he partnered Sidwell to win the American doubles and the doubles match in the challenge round of the Davis Cup. In 1950 he partnered Sedgman in both—and won both again. Bromwich won the mixed doubles at Wimbledon with Miss Brough in 1947 and 1948, and they won the American mixed in 1947. Whoever partnered Bromwich always appeared to the spectators to be crashing home winning volleys and smashes. But the acute observer knew quite well that the openings were made by the uncanny accuracy and acute tactical sense of John Bromwich.

Miss Hart was back again, quite recovered from her eye injury, to contest the women's singles once more. Britain could only provide one seeded player, Mrs. C. Harrison (Betty Hilton), who was competing on her honeymoon and not taking tennis too seriously. Nevertheless she was the only British player to survive to the last eight. Miss Brough lost a set to Miss Fry; Miss Hart routed Miss Scofield; Mrs. Todd had a comfortable win against Mrs. Harrison; and Mrs. du Pont lost eight games to Miss Moran—who this year was concentrating more on the tennis. Miss Brough played brilliantly to stave off Miss Hart's challenge in two straight sets, and Mrs. du Pont had to fight every inch of the way to beat the very gallant Mrs. Todd 8–6, 4–6, 8–6. Mrs. du Pont had had a long and distinguished career in the top ranks of world lawn tennis, and this year for the first time seemed to be definitely slower about the court than she had been and to be placing more reliance on the defensive chop than on the attacking drive. She won the middle set from Miss Brough but could then only take one game in the decider.

In the ladies' doubles two British pairs came through to the last eight; Mrs. Rita Anderson and Miss Joan Curry, and Mrs. Harrison and Miss Tuckey. Mrs. Mottram also came through in partnership with Mrs. Long of Australia. Mrs. Anderson and Miss Curry went out in straight sets to Miss Fry and Miss Hart; Mrs. Long and Mrs. Mottram beat Miss Moran and Mrs. Todd in three sets; and Mrs. Buck and Miss Chaffee beat Mrs. Harrison and Miss Tuckey much too easily for the prestige of British doubles. In the final Miss Brough and Mrs. du Pont triumphed for the third year running, though Miss Fry and Miss Hart took the middle set. Miss Brough, this time partnered by Eric Sturgess of South Africa, won the mixed doubles.

Since the challenge round was abolished in 1922 only Mrs.

Helen Wills-Moody had, previous to Miss Brough, succeeded in winning the singles title three years running, and once again Miss Brough joined the ranks of the immortals in winning all three events at one Wimbledon.

Mrs. du Pont made a magnificent comeback to win the American singles title, and for the ninth time running she and Miss Brough won the doubles—surely a record which will never be beaten. Mrs. du Pont also won the mixed with K. McGregor of Australia, thereby winning the triple crown and going out of big tennis in a blaze of glory. The men's singles championship of America was won by A. Larsen, and the doubles, for the second year running, went to an Australian pair, John Bromwich and Frank Sedgman.

In the 1951 Australian Championships, played at Melbourne in January, R. Savitt (U.S.A.) beat McGregor in the final of the singles in four sets; Sedgman and McGregor beat the holders, Quist and Bromwich, in a stern five-set doubles final; and Mrs. Nancye Bolton scored her sixth win in the National singles.

There was a particularly strong entry for the 1951 British Hard Court Championships. Jaroslav Drobny, a supreme artist on hard courts, won the men's event as he pleased— neither Mottram nor Paish managing to reach the semi-final, though Paish played the match of his life in taking Eric Sturgess to five sets. Norgarb and Sturgess won the men's doubles for South Africa after a tough five-set battle in the semi-final with Mottram and Paish.

In the women's singles Mrs. Walker-Smith put up a fine performance in beating Mrs. Bolton, the Australian champion, for the loss of only two games, then overcoming the ambidexterous Miss Beverly Baker of the U.S.A., and finally pressing Miss Doris Hart all the way in the final. Miss Fry and Miss Hart won the women's doubles, and Sturgess and Miss Hart the mixed.

In the 1951 French Championship Drobny won the men's singles, and Miss Fry the women's. The brilliant Australian pair, McGregor and Sedgman, won the men's doubles, and Miss Hart and Miss Fry won the women's doubles for the second year running.

There were some noteworthy newcomers to the 1951

Wimbledon—Herbert Flam (U.S.A.), who had been runner-up to Larsen in the 1950 American Championship at Forest Hills; Richard Savitt (U.S.A.), the Australian champion(38); and seventeen-year-old Hamilton Richardson (U.S.A.), who was reckoned to be one of the most promising youngsters in the world. On the women's side there was the ambidexterous Miss Beverly Baker, ranked Number 4 in the States, and the American negress, Miss Althea Gibson.

The seeded players for the men's singles included two Australians, Frank Sedgman and Ken McGregor; five Americans, G. Mulloy, H. Flam, A. Larsen, R. Savitt and Budge Patty; also Eric Sturgess of South Africa, L. Bergelin of Sweden and J. Drobny, now of Egypt. Drobny, who was seeded second to Frank Sedgman, had been so devastating on hard courts that many people thought that this was at last to be his lucky year.

There was the usual galaxy of stars in the women's events, including Miss Brough, the Wimbledon holder, and Mrs. du Pont, the American reigning champion. But Miss Brough had a sore elbow, and I felt that Mrs. du Pont must at last have passed her peak. So, not without some inside knowledge, I plumped this year for Miss Doris Hart in my pre-Wimbledon article in the *Sunday Times*.

In the men's singles the first big upset was a great victory for Britain's Tony Mottram over the second seed, Jaroslav Drobny, at 8–6 in the final set of an exciting five-set match. It must be admitted that Drobny was suffering from a slightly strained shoulder, but he reached the final of the men's doubles, so there could not have been very much the matter with him. However, the ever enigmatic Mottram faded away completely in the next round, only getting three games from the Swedish stylist, L. Bergelin.

The second big upset was the second-round defeat of the holder, Budge Patty, by the American junior champion, seventeen-year-old Hamilton Richardson, in a long five-set match. Hamilton Richardson's modest demeanour on court made him an instant favourite with the Wimbledon crowd, and Patty took his unexpected defeat as sportingly as any champion possibly could have done in such circumstances.

Frank Sedgman, having won the first two sets with ease,

went out to the pertinacious Herbie Flam. Larsen, the American champion, was almost routed by Savitt. Sturgess came through easily against A. Vieira of Brazil, and McGregor just outlasted Bergelin.

In the semi-final Savitt, having survived a 15–13 second set, beat Flam, and McGregor somewhat surprisingly beat Sturgess. The final was rather poor. McGregor's only chance against a much superior stroke player was to use his big service and telescopic reach in a Borotra-like net assault. But he was unaccountably nervous and tentative, and by the time he got into the match it was safely in Savitt's pocket.

Savitt was a big heavy man with a curiously highly strung nervous temperament, but with great determination and every shot in his bag—particularly a most punishing and accurate topspin backhand drive. To give of his best he had to be trained to the minute—as he was at this Wimbledon. When he was not completely fit he was apt to be slow on his feet, but he was certainly a very fine player and a very worthy Wimbledon champion.

In the men's doubles one of the four seeds, H. Flam and A. Larsen of the United States, went out in the first round to Sweden's fine Davis Cup pair, Lennart Bergelin and Sven Davidson, who were the best doubles team in Europe. Britain's Davis Cup pair of Mottram and Paish went down to their old enemies, G. Cucelli and M. del Bello of Italy, rather tamely. Evidence of the post-war lawn tennis weakness of Great Britain in the doubles game was the fact that not a single British pair reached the last sixteen. The finalists were the very strong Australian pair, Ken McGregor and Frank Sedgman, and Jaroslav Drobny and Eric Sturgess. Sturgess played a magnificent game in the final with rather poor support from his partner who was obviously not completely fit. The Australians took five sets to win; but one never felt they could lose.

The only two British players to reach the last eight of the women's singles were Mrs. Walker-Smith and Miss Kay Tuckey. The next round saw the exit of one of the "Queens" —a most unprecedented event at this stage of a post-war Wimbledon. Mrs. du Pont, who in the round before against the good British left-hander, Mrs. Dawson-Scott, had shown distinct signs of nerves, was well beaten in three sets by the ambidexterous Miss Beverly Baker. Miss Nancy Chaffee, a lovely stroke maker in both senses of the words, failed to produce enough concentration to extend Miss Doris Hart. Mrs. Walker-Smith fought most gallantly against the new champion of France, Miss Shirley Fry, and only lost 6–8, 4–6. Miss Tuckey won the first set against Miss Brough, who was obviously in pain from her injured arm, but then faded out badly when she looked a winner. This was a gallant effort on the part of Miss Brough, but she couldn't repeat it in the next round against Miss Fry, who won 6–4, 6–2. Miss Hart beat Miss Baker very convincingly, and so the new doubles champions of France faced one another in the final. For Miss Hart it was one of those days when she could do no wrong, and when she was in that form she was irresistible. These two had recently met in the final of the French Championships, when Miss Fry had won in three sets. But on the fast turf of the Centre Court it was a different story. Not since the days of Suzanne Lenglen had any woman given a more perfect display of tennis than Miss Hart produced to win 6–1, 6–0 in the space of thirty-five minutes. The power and accuracy of her service and the fine length and pace of her ground strokes battered Miss Fry's defences to pieces, until they were pierced from every quarter. After twice being runner-up, Miss Hart was at last the singles champion—and seldom has there been one more popular or more gallant.

Despite their wonderful doubles record, few people expected Miss Brough and Mrs. du Pont to retain their championship. That they reached the final and then only went down to Miss Hart and Miss Fry 3–6, 11–13 is a tribute both to their wonderful class as a pair and to their courage in adversity. Three British pairs reached the last eight. Mrs. Mottram and Mrs. Walker-Smith failed to make any impression on the holders; Mrs. Dawson-Scott and Miss Wilford, who always gave a good account of themselves at Wimbledon, lost to Mrs. Davidson and Miss Rosenquest of the U.S.A., 6–8, 1–6. Miss Eyre and Miss V. S. White, who had done well to get so far, went out in straight sets to Miss Baker and Miss Chaffee; and Miss Quertier and Miss Tuckey, of whom much was expected, could only get four games from

Miss Hart and Miss Fry. The latter then slaughtered Miss Baker and Miss Chaffee for the loss of only two games, and the holders, Miss Brough and Mrs. du Pont, won easily against Mrs. Davidson and Miss Rosenquest.

The year before Miss Hart and Miss Fry had only been able to take a set from Miss Brough and Mrs. du Pont in the final. This year they got off to a flying start and won the first set 6–3 after twenty minutes play. In the second set the champions showed something of their former greatness and led 5–2, with the younger pair ragged and anxious. But the holders failed to keep their lead and finally were overwhelmed and beaten. Had they managed to win that set I believe they would have won the match, despite Miss Brough's arm and Mrs. du Pont's obvious loss of form. It was sad to see the great pair beaten—and to feel that it was probably their swan-song. They scratched from the American Championships, and Miss Brough appeared the next year with a new partner. During the first six years of post-war lawn tennis in Britain these two Queens of the court, Miss Brough and Mrs. du Pont, had played a leading part every year, generally staying long enough to play in one or two tournaments as well as Wimbledon. They always played at Queen's Club in both singles and doubles, and in whatever event they played they gave of their very best. They had no mannerisms on court and no eccentricities of dress. They both looked charming in plain, well-cut dresses or shorts—and after all "handsome is as handsome does", and they were certainly models both in their appearance and in their play.

Of all the great women champions I can remember they were the least conceited, the least temperamental and the easiest to deal with. When the referee said "play" they were ready to go on court however bad the conditions or the weather and however tired they might be. They had the will to win strongly developed, as all great champions must have, and they never under-estimated their opponents or played down to them. They were great ornaments to the game they loved, great ambassadors for the United States, and as popular a couple as ever set foot on the sacred turf of Wimbledon. Their triumphs were world-wide as was their welcome.

Miss Hart won the mixed doubles with Frank Sedgman, and so joined the three immortals—Suzanne Lenglen, Alice Marble and Louise Brough, who had won all three events at the same Wimbledon.

The ascendancy attained by Australia in the men's doubles game was again demonstrated in the American Championships, held at the Longwood Cricket Club, Boston, in August. William Talbert and Gardnar Mulloy, the famous American doubles pair who had won the title four times, were defeated in the semi-final by the second string Australian combination of Mervyn Rose and Don Candy in a terrific match 6–4, 6–8, 20–18, 9–7. In the other semi-final the Australian top pair, Frank Sedgman and Kenneth McGregor, holders of the British, Australian and French doubles titles, routed Budge Patty and Tony Trabert 6–3, 6–1, 6–4 in a perfect exhibition of the doubles game. For the first two sets Sedgman hardly made a single error, and was altogether quite devastating. Candy and Rose put up a spirited resistance to their senior pair in the final, and only went down 8–10, 4–6, 6–4, 5–7.

Miss Nancy Chaffee and Mrs. Pat Todd defeated the British combination of Jean Quertier and Kay Tuckey 6–3, 6–3, and Miss Fry and Miss Hart beat the other British pair, Mrs. Mottram and Miss Ward 6–3, 6–2. Miss Fry and Miss Hart won the final comfortably, and so added the American title to the French and British.

The outstanding features of the American National Championships at Forest Hills, which followed in early September, was the brilliant singles play of Frank Sedgman (44) and the sixteen-year-old American girl, Miss Maureen Connolly (45). The most outstanding match in the fourth round of the men's singles was that between Art Larsen, the holder, and his young compatriot, Hamilton Richardson. The latter very nearly added the scalp of the American holder to that of Budge Patty, the Wimbledon holder, which he had lifted at Wimbledon. At five-all in the fifth set play had to be called off for the day owing to bad light, and when play was restarted Larsen clinched the match in a few minutes. Savitt was suffering from a boil on his leg and, after gallantly defeating Budge Patty at 6–4 in the fifth set, went out to Victor Seixas, who had been taken the full distance by

Herbert Flam. In the quarter-finals Sedgman beat Tony Trabert 3–6, 6–2, 7–5, 3–6, 6–3 in his only hard match throughout the event. But in his last two matches the Australian beat Larsen, the holder, 6–1, 6–2, 6–0, and then Victor Seixas in the final 6–4, 6–1, 6–1. I have never seen a more devastating performance than Sedgman's in these two matches. He was really almost unplayable. Larsen's defeat in forty-nine minutes play was the worst upset ever suffered by a title holder in the American Championships. And Sedgman's defeat of Seixas in the final in forty-eight minutes was just as crushing. With the exception of one previous defeat by Sedgman, Seixas had not suffered a single defeat the whole season. But he was powerless to combat the fury of Sedgman's attack. Serving magnificently himself and standing well inside the baseline to receive his opponent's powerful delivery, Sedgman was on top of the net in a flash, and, once there, his volleys and smashes were absolutely lethal. The packed stadium crowd were absolutely spellbound and almost too astonished to clap until it was all over, when they gave the twenty-three-year-old Australian a tremendous ovation.

So Sedgman became the first Australian to win the American singles championship in the seventy years the tournament had been held. In doing so he only lost two sets—both of them to Tony Trabert. Sedgman was the fifth foreign player ever to win the American title—the others being H. L. Doherty (Great Britain) in 1903, Rene Lacoste (France) in 1926 and 1927, Henri Cochet (France) in 1928, and F. J. Perry (Great Britain) in 1933, 1934 and 1936.

Sedgman, in partnership with Miss Doris Hart, with whom he had won at Wimbledon, added the mixed doubles to the men's singles, and men's doubles.

In the absence of Mrs. du Pont, the holder, and Miss Louise Brough, Miss Doris Hart, the Wimbledon winner, was confidently expected to win her first American championship, though I had described her play in the Wightman Cup match just before as tentative and nervy. In the United States there is a separate seeding list for United States and foreign players. In the U.S.A. list Miss Hart was seeded first, and was followed by Miss Fry, Mrs. Todd, Miss Connolly, Miss Chaffee,

Miss Beverly Baker and Miss Rosenquest. The foreign list consisted entirely of the British Wightman Cup team who had just been defeated by the American women by six matches to one.

A minor sensation was caused by the United States Lawn Tennis Association just before the event started when they announced officially that they would not countenance any daring and "questionable fashion displays" on court. They had already applied this ruling to a young lady umpire who had taken the chair in a strapless gown and been asked to retire and add something to her costume. This action by the U.S.L.T.A. was the result of some of the rather daring tennis dresses seen at Wimbledon.

Miss Helen Fletcher, the young British left-hander who had had a disappointing début in the States, went out in the first round to the non-playing captain of the U.S. Wightman Cup team, Mrs. "Midge" Buck. Mrs. Walker-Smith had great difficulty in disposing of Mrs. Lewis (U.S.A.) in the third round. Miss Tuckey brought off her best performance in defeating Miss Beverly Baker to enter the quarter-finals, and Miss Quertier played brilliantly to beat Miss Head (U.S.A.) by 6–1, 6–0. I doubt whether any other player in the world could have beaten Miss Head so convincingly. In the quarter-finals Mrs. Walker-Smith enhanced her reputation by an excellent straight-set win over Mrs. Rurac; and Miss Fry only beat Miss Tuckey 9–7, 3–6, 6–2 in a match which Miss Tuckey really should have won in two sets. Miss Quertier, of whom so much was expected, never looked like holding Miss Connolly and was always on the defensive in her 3–6, 3–6 defeat. And Miss Hart had too much concentration for the scintillating Miss Chaffee, whose strokes were as always a joy to watch. When Mrs. Walker-Smith won the first set of her semi-final match against Miss Fry 6–2 we began to calculate when we had last had a British player in the finals of this championship. But alas, when it came to a final set Miss Fry had too much stamina and experience, as she had shown in similar circumstances against Miss Tuckey. And in the other semi-final, wonder of wonders, sixteen-year-old Maureen Connolly(45), the fabulous "Little Mo" of the nodding head and twinkling feet put out the favourite, Miss

Doris Hart, 6–4, 6–4. But behind that bare statement of the score quite a lot of drama was hidden.

When the players went on court the heat wave, which had made even watching tennis almost unbearable, had passed, dark clouds were rolling up and rain appeared imminent. Miss Hart started strongly and was very soon leading 4–0. Then a few drops of rain fell and she lost some of her concentration. Her young opponent, always more courageous and more dangerous when she is down, launched a fierce counter-attack from the baseline cheered on by the crowd, which, like any other crowd, encourages the player who is behind. More rain started to fall; the stricken Miss Hart looked fearfully at the sky and hopefully at the umpire; and, whilst both were undecided, Miss Connolly had won six games off the reel to take the first set—as the heavens opened and the rain came down in torrents. It was a brave effort on Miss Connolly's part, but a disastrous upset and rather cruel luck for Miss Hart.

Next day the match was resumed in bright sunshine but with the court surface still damp—and Miss Hart never quite trusts her foothold on a slippery court. From the start little Maureen went all out at her opponent like a boxer in the ring who has put his man down once and doesn't intend to let him recover. Miss Hart bowed before the storm and was soon 1–5 down and on the verge of defeat. Then she staged as gallant a rally as anyone could wish to see to pull up to 4–5 and come within a point of 5–5. I felt that if she could just have got that one more point the championship would yet have been hers. But the strain had been too great against an opponent who fought for every point. The tenth game and the match went to Miss Connolly. Both players were in tears when they left the court. It had been a heart-breaking disappointment for Miss Hart, who, with Miss Brough and Mrs. du Pont in the lists against her, had yet been a finalist three times and now, with both her great rivals removed from her path, had fallen to a sixteen-year-old girl.

But the stalwart Miss Fry, champion over Doris Hart in France and runner-up at Wimbledon, still stood in the way. Her plan of campaign was obvious from the start; she was going to wage a war of attrition from the baseline, slowing down the game all she knew and forcing Maureen to make her own pace. And how very near it came to success, and how very near she was to reducing her small opponent to complete frustration and exhaustion! But in the crisis of the third set it was apparent that Miss Fry was much the more exhausted of the two.

> *The man recovered from the bite*
> *The dog it was that died.*

Unutterably weary from her long self-imposed defensive chase, the gallant Miss Fry could scarcely move her feet or raise her racket as little twinkle toes, sensing her opportunity, came in for the kill with a smash, drop shot and flashing backhand drive which gave her the championship of the United States.

Like Helen Wills-Moody before her, Miss Connolly had built her game on the firm foundation of deep, speedy accurate ground strokes, perfected by unremitting practice and supported by neat and balanced footwork and an exceptionally tough physique, strengthened by skipping and a lot of actual play, much of it against male opponents.

The 1952 season started with the Australian National Championships in January. Dick Savitt of the U.S.A., the holder, and also the Wimbledon champion, stayed on after the Davis Cup match to defend his championship. He reached the semi-final, and then lost to Ken McGregor, who most unexpectedly beat Frank Sedgman in the final to gain his first national championship.

These upsets in form amongst the world's leading players would seem extraordinary to anyone who did not realise the strain of modern tennis and how easily the weather and other extraneous factors can affect results.

The 1952 British Hard Court Championship at Bournemouth attracted a really magnificent entry, including the holder, Jaroslav Drobny, who was reckoned to be the world's finest player on hard courts, and Frank Sedgman of Australia, the American champion, ranked on his 1951 performances as the world's leading player on grass. Other leading Australian players who had entered were Don Candy and I. Ayre. The

British players, Mottram and Paish, John Horn and young R. Becker were all competing. Besides all the leading British players, the two leading Americans, Miss Hart and Miss Fry, the Wimbledon champion and runner-up, were playing in the ladies' events.

In the men's singles Becker did very well to run the strong Australian, Ayre, to 8–10, 6–8, 4–6 in the third round. In the quarter-finals Candy beat Mottram in four sets; Ayre beat Horn very easily; and Drobny, who lost five games in his first three matches, only allowed Paish one of them. Drobny, however, lost a set in the semi-final, and Britain's Gerry Oakley distinguished himself by taking a set from Sedgman. The final between Sedgman and Drobny was expected to be a thrilling encounter. Drobny, who had just lost twice to Sedgman on rubble, was in full training and eager to win. Sedgman, on the other hand, was on a honeymoon tour and had been on court the night before up to a late hour in a long mixed doubles match in which he nearly pulled his charming bride through against a first-class pair. It was certainly not the best preparation for a championship single the next day, but on hard courts, made particularly slow by heavy rain, Drobny was the supreme master he can be under those conditions, and one set was all Sedgman could get.

In the women's singles Britain's covered court champion, Miss Susan Partridge, played well to beat Miss Pat Ward for the loss of only three games, and to run Miss Hart to 3–6, 8–10. Mrs. Walker-Smith reached the semi-final and took seven games from Miss Hart. Mrs. Mottram did extremely well to beat Mrs. Rinkel-Quertier 6–3, 6–1, but could make little impression on Miss Fry in the semi-final. In the final Miss Hart beat Miss Fry in straight sets, both playing tired and mechanical tennis after their long world tour. Mottram and Paish gave a fine exhibition to beat the strong Australian combination of Candy and Ayre in five sets, but, somewhat naturally, could make little impression on Drobny and Sedgman in the final.

In the women's doubles the British Wightman Cup players, Miss Fletcher and Miss Ward, who had had the benefit of several months coaching in America, paired together with considerable success. They beat Mrs. Mottram and Mrs. Walker-Smith in two sets, and in the semi-final only went down to Miss Partridge and Mrs. Rinkel-Quertier at 6–8 in the final set. The latter pair took five games from Miss Hart and Miss Fry in the final.

In the last week in May the world's leading players gathered to do battle in the French National Championships on the courts of the Stade Roland Garros in Paris. This is probably the most arduous tournament in the world as it is as long as Wimbledon, but the slow pace of the courts makes encounters between equally matched players protracted affairs; and it is much more difficult to put the ball away than it is on the fast grass of Wimbledon. Also the surface is much harder on the feet than grass.

In the men's singles Britain's Tony Mottram won a meritorious victory in five sets over a much improved young American, G. Golden, but was then beaten in straight sets by the Italian star, F. Gardini.

Australia delivered her strongest possible challenge with her three top players, Sedgman, McGregor and Mervyn Rose, and a couple of newcomers to international tennis in the shape of two seventeen-year-olds, Rosewall and Hoad. These two youngsters, so unlike in style and appearance, created an instant impression and had a remarkable first year in big tennis. Rosewall, small, slight and dark, is a stylist and a tactician with a good head on his shoulders. Hoad is burly and fair, with a crashing service and thumping volleys. Both have cool temperaments and immense resource and courage in tight places. They owe much to the stern but imaginative coaching of that great Davis Cup captain, Harry Hopman.

The American challenge was delivered by the Wimbledon champion, R. Savitt; Tony Trabert, who had run Sedgman so close at Forest Hills; Budge Patty, the 1950 Wimbledon champion; the veteran Gardnar Mulloy, who was to have an amazingly successful year; and young Hamilton Richardson, who had made such a sensational début in international tennis in 1951.

And in addition there were Eric Sturgess of South Africa, always a fine hard court exponent; K. Nielsen of Denmark;

and first and foremost the holder, J. Drobny, who was quite rightly reckoned to be the greatest hard court player in the world.

Young Rosewall played quite magnificently to run the Italian, Gardini, to five sets, and Hoad only went down to Sturgess 7-9, 6-8, 4-6. These two Australian youngsters were obviously going to be a menace to the world's best players. Nielsen came through a long five-setter with Nigel Cockburn of South Africa, only to go out to Sedgman in straight sets. Budge Patty overcame the Italian, R. del Bello, but could not get a set from Sedgman. Savitt, after coming within a point of winning, was run to a standstill by Eric Sturgess, as fit a player as there has even been. Trabert, who was doing his Naval Service and was out of practice, was beaten by the diminutive little Philippino, F. Ampon, who in turn was overwhelmed by the gigantic McGregor in the next round. Drobny defeated Gardini and G. Mulloy with masterly ease and reached the final after beating McGregor in four sets. Sturgess had reached the semi-final of this championship for the sixth successive year, but then found Sedgman too much for him. So once again in the space of a few weeks Drobny and Sedgman faced one another across the net in the final of a hard court championship. And once again the weather favoured Drobny, as rain had made the courts slower than usual, which handicapped Sedgman's essentially all-court hustling game. But Drobny is undoubtedly a most exceptional hard court player. The slower surface gives his uncanny control of the drop shot and wonderful topspin lob full scope, and in addition he has the big guns of a great service and tremendous whipped forehand drive. Of all the great players on hard courts I have ever seen from Tilden, Lacoste and Cochet downwards, I would rank Drobny very high indeed. He beat Sedgman for the loss of only eleven games, much as he had done at Bournemouth.

Britain was represented in the women's singles by Mrs. Mottram, Miss Joan Curry, Miss Pat Ward and Miss Susan Partridge. Mrs. Mottram and Miss Curry reached the quarter-finals, where the former lost in an exciting three-set struggle to Miss Dorothy Head (U.S.A.), and Miss Curry

38 R. Savitt, Wimbledon
champion of 1951

39 R. A. Gonzales, American
champion 1948-9

40 J. A. Kramer, Wimbledon
champion 1947 and American
champion 1946-7

41 F. R. Schroeder, Wimbledon
champion 1949 and American
champion 1942

42 Jaroslav Drobny, who twice reached the final at Wimbledon

43 Eric Sturgess (South Africa) who narrowly missed the big championships after World War II

went out to Miss Fry after winning the first set. Miss Curry was always hard to beat on the French courts and had a victory to her credit there over the great Louise Brough. But how many times had British players gone down to the Americans when it came to a final set! What was the reason? Was it food? Or something else? I don't believe it was lack of skill—and certainly not a lack of the quality vulgarly known as "guts". But I shall have more to say on this subject in a later chapter. The inevitable Miss Hart and Miss Fry reached the final, and Miss Hart reversed the previous year's decision by winning 6–4, 6–4.

In the ladies' doubles Miss Fry and Miss Hart scored the easiest of victories, and the world beating Australian pair, Sedgman and McGregor, added the men's championship to their other laurels. Mention must be made of the wonderful play of the veteran Jean Borotra in this event. With his compatriot, R. Abdesselam, he beat Nielsen and Ulrich, the strong Danish Davis Cup pair, in an exhausting five-set match and then took the Americans, Gardnar Mulloy and Savitt, to a fifth set before finally acknowledging defeat. What a player Jean Borotra was!

And so the stage began to be set for the 1952 Wimbledon— the seventy-fifth anniversary of the championships. On the men's side the main interest centred around the expected duel between Jaroslav Drobny, the outstanding artist on hard courts, and the premier player in the world on grass, Frank Sedgman of Australia. And on the women's side Great Britain was agog over the first appearance on English courts of little Maureen Connolly, champion of the United States. Was her victory there just a flash in the pan, and would she really have any chance of wresting the Wimbledon title from the holder, Miss Doris Hart, who had appeared with such distinction on British courts every year since the war?

Miss Connolly made her first public appearance at the Surbiton tournament in the last week of May. She was opposed by two formidable opponents in Mrs. Thelma Long of Australia and Mrs. Pat Todd of the United States, the latter of whom had defeated her several times before and was quite confident of doing so again. But Miss Connolly showed all the qualities of a real champion in defeating both these opponents when all the run of the play was against her. As I had predicted a year before, she won the hearts of the British crowd by her naturalness, her desire to give of her best, her will to win—and the excellence of her play.

The seeded players for Wimbledon in the men's singles were: 1. F. A. Sedgman (Australia); 2. Jaroslav Drobny (Egypt); 3. V. Seixas (U.S.A.); 4. R. Savitt (U.S.A.); 5. K. McGregor (Australia); 6. H. Flam (U.S.A.); 7. E. W. Sturgess (South Africa); 8. Mervyn Rose (Australia); 9. A. Larsen (U.S.A.); 10. Gardnar Mulloy (U.S.A.); 11. H. Richardson (U.S.A.); 12. Budge Patty (U.S.A.).

Only two British players reached the last thirty-two. Tony Mottram overcame his old enemy, G. Cucelli of Italy, but, as usual, could make no impression on Eric Sturgess; and John Horn was quite outclassed by Budge Patty. Hamilton Richardson (U.S.A.) went out in the first round to F. Ampon. In the fourth round Sedgman beat his compatriot, D. Candy, for the loss of only three games; Sturgess had a very close call against young Golden of the United States and was somewhat lucky to win; Budge Patty went down to Victor Seixas in four sets; and Drobny lost a set to young Hoad of Australia. In the quarter-finals Sedgman overwhelmed Sturgess; Mervyn Rose outlasted and beat the slightly under-trained holder, R. Savitt, in a magnificent match; Flam rather unexpectedly beat Seixas for the loss of one set; and Drobny had a nerve-shattering five-set match to beat McGregor.

In the semi-final Sedgman beat Rose in straight sets, and Drobny had another very close call against the pertinacious Herbie Flam of the U.S.A. What a grand fighter Flam is! Without a quarter of the weapons of Drobny he yet, by his sheer courage and refusal to admit defeat, reduced his more accomplished opponent to a state of nervous frazzle which very nearly defeated him completely.

Drobny had every chance of beating Sedgman in the final as he won the first set and was in his best form. But when tackled with the full determination of an all-out offensive Drobny wilted, went back on to the defensive and could only get seven games in the last three sets. Drobny had been seeded five times at Wimbledon, out of his eight appearances, and on several occasions had been expected to win. What was the reason for his constant failure at the critical moment? Up to 1950 I think the main reason was the fact that he had one weak stroke in his armoury—a sliced backhand that was a gift to the strong attacking net player. He then corrected this weakness and appeared to be armed at all points. He had wonderful physique and a formidable array of strokes, his service, smash and forehand drive being outstanding weapons in the whole history of lawn tennis. I would put his Wimbledon failures down to two causes—firstly, he played too much and did not concentrate on the main championship. Secondly, although the winning of Wimbledon was his supreme ambition, he did not—certainly in 1951 and 1952—take anything like the trouble to get himself into the necessary physical and nervous condition for victory that his particular temperament required. Had he, for instance, trained as Anthony Wilding did from a quiet lodging house in Wimbledon close to the courts Drobny would, I believe, have won two Wimbledon Championships.

In the men's doubles Britain's leading pair, Mottram and Paish, distinguished themselves greatly by reaching the last eight. They had a most meritorious win in the first round over the Australian pair, Candy and Rose, who had reached the American finals at Boston the year before, and they went out eventually to Drobny and Budge Patty, after having very nearly won the match in the fourth set. But the fact that the British pair could only get one game when it came to a fifth set again showed up our lack of finishing power. The holders, McGregor and Sedgman, lost a set to Flam and Larsen, and also, in the quarter-finals, to the Italian pair, G. Cucelli and M. del Bello. Seixas and Sturgess, a new partnership, took five sets to defeat Ayre and Hamilton Richardson. The young Australians, Hoad and Rosewall, played really magnificently to beat first Mulloy and Savitt, and then Morea and Russell. Seixas and Sturgess, playing all they knew, were lucky to beat the young Australians in the semi-final round. The latter certainly had the wholehearted support of a very fair Wimbledon crowd.

McGregor and Sedgman beat Seixas and Sturgess in the final in straight sets—this being their seventh successive victory in the world's major doubles championships.

~ 143 ~

The seeded players in the ladies' singles were: 1. Miss Hart; 2. Miss Connolly; 3. Miss Fry; 4. Miss Brough; 5. Mrs. Todd; 6. Mrs. Walker-Smith; 7. Mrs. Long; 8. Mrs. Rinkel-Quertier.

Miss Hart was eager to retain her championship and prove that the result at Forest Hills was all wrong; Miss Connolly was eager to show her best form on her first visit to Britain and prove that her Forest Hills form was all right; Miss Fry wanted to improve her position as the eternal second; and Miss Brough wanted to make a much more champion-like bow to Wimbledon than her injured arm had permitted her to do the year before. Mrs. Todd, the greatest fighter of them all, was just out for anybody's blood, and, as far as she was concerned, the higher they were the harder they would fall.

A few days before the championships started Miss Connolly suffered a minor injury to her arm in practice. This little upset, combined with all the ballyhoo which surrounds such a person on these occasions, worked up such an emotional atmosphere between "Little Mo" and her entourage that she very nearly was persuaded to scratch. But her own good sense and sportsmanship eventually prevailed. However, she was far below her Forest Hills form to start with, and would have lost to Britain's Miss Partridge in the fourth round had the latter grasped her opportunity when leading a sorely worried opponent in all the critical stages of the final set. Miss Connolly then lost a set to Mrs. Long of Australia before reaching the semi-final. Britain's leading player, Mrs. Walker-Smith, reached the last eight and then was beaten all ends up by Miss Fry. Mrs. Rinkel-Quertier also reached the last eight and then went down in two sets to Miss Brough.

The gallant Pat Todd brought off her greatest singles triumph when she beat the holder, Miss Hart, 6-8, 7-5, 6-4. The intense heat and Mrs. Todd's tremendous fighting spirit wore down Miss Hart's nervous and physical reserves. But it had been obvious for nearly a year that her constant tournaments all over the world had made her stale and nervy. Had Miss Hart parcelled out her physical and nervous resources more wisely she would have won the American championship of 1951 and the Wimbledon title of 1952.

The two winners of the British and American singles titles for 1952

44   Frank   Sedgman
(Australia)

45   Miss   Maureen
Connolly("Little Mo")
(U.S.A.)

46 The Davis Cup comes back to Britain in 1933 after twenty-two years. F. J. Perry (*left*) beats A. Merlin (France) in the deciding match in Paris

Miss Brough lost a set in beating Mrs. Todd, and it was like old times to see her contesting the final again; but the old fire and fury of her game had gone, and, try as she would, she could not counter the stream of hard hit drives that flowed from Maureen's racket. All power then to the little champion who, in spite of being badgered and bewildered by a crowd of hangers-on, which reminded me of a Sugar Ray Robinson tour, kept her head cool and her courage high and achieved her life's ambition of being Wimbledon champion.

In the ladies' doubles Britain had no less than five pairs in the quarter-finals. Miss Eyre and Miss White, who had distinguished themselves by reaching this position the year before, went out to Miss Brough and Miss Connolly. Mrs. Blair and Mrs. Halford succumbed to Mrs. Long and Mrs. Todd. Miss Partridge and Mrs. Rinkel-Quertier, the only seeded British pair, beat Miss Fletcher and Mrs. Walker-Smith in three sets, and Miss Bulleid and Miss Mortimer lost to Miss Hart and Miss Fry.

In the final Miss Brough's great knowledge and power were not sufficient to bring her young partner, as yet inexperienced in the doubles game, through to victory against such a stream-lined combination as Miss Hart and Miss Fry, who for the best part of two years had won all the major doubles prizes in the world.

The holders, Sedgman and Miss Hart, won the mixed—Sedgman thereby winning the triple crown.

In the American doubles championships in August the Australians, McGregor and Sedgman, were beaten for the first time in two years by an untried partnership of V. Seixas (U.S.A.) and Mervyn Rose (Australia); but, in fairness to the Australians, McGregor had been suffering from a strained stomach muscle which eventually caused his retirement from the national singles at Forest Hills.

Miss Fry and Miss Hart won the women's doubles for the second year in succession, though they only managed to beat Miss Brough and Miss Connolly 10–8, 6–4 in the final. The only British pair, Miss Fletcher and Miss Mortimer, did excellently to reach the semi-final round of this event. Mrs. "Midge" Buck, the American Wightman Cup captain, won her fourth successive veterans singles championship and won the veterans doubles with Mrs. Hazel Wightman, the donor of the Wightman Cup. This was Mrs. Wightman's forty-third national championship—a really fabulous achievement.

In the national singles championships of America, Frank Sedgman and Maureen Connolly retained their titles. Sedgman was even more supreme than he had been the year before and won without the loss of a set. The two Australian youngsters, Hoad and Rosewall, reached the quarter-finals and the latter then very nearly defeated the American finalist, Gardnar Mulloy, who at his eighteenth attempt got farther than ever before—which is certainly a great tribute to his physical fitness.

But possibly the finest performance of the whole year was Ken Rosewall's defeat of Vic Seixas, America's top player, in the fourth round. How delighted we should have been in Britain if we could have produced a seventeen-year-old with anything like this wonderful performance and promise.

The women's singles went according to form, with Miss Connolly, Miss Hart, Miss Fry and Miss Brough reaching the semi-final. Miss Brough harassed Miss Hart all the way, and only lost 7–9, 6–8, and Miss Connolly dropped the first set to Miss Fry. But Miss Hart only got eight games in the final against Miss Connolly, which was exactly the number she got the year before.

The mixed doubles were won by Sedgman and Miss Hart, who had established themselves as the world's finest exponents of this type of game.

In the first week of October the International Clubs of France and Great Britain met at Queen's Club for their annual encounter on covered courts. This match was notable for Jean Borotra's thirty-fourth successive appearance, in London or Paris, and in his fifty-fifth year he was still good enough to give twenty-two years and a beating to Britain's Number 1 player, Tony Mottram.

In the covered court championship which followed the I.C. match Drobny beat Mottram in the men's final, and Miss Partridge lost her women's title to the steadily improving Miss Angela Mortimer. Mottram and Paish scored an excellent victory in five sets over Drobny and Williams in the men's doubles final, and Mrs. Rinkel-Quertier and Miss

Fletcher triumphed over Miss Bulleid and Miss Mortimer in the women's doubles.

That excellent British mixed doubles pair, Paish and Mrs. Rinkel-Quertier, won the mixed doubles.

As always, towards the end of the year, the focus of the lawn tennis world's attention was fixed upon the challenge round of the Davis Cup, played again this year in the country of the holders, Australia, which I have described in another chapter.

There had been many changes and improvements made at Wimbledon since the championships started again after the Second World War. The war damage was, of course, repaired and the full seating capacity of the Centre Court restored. The entries for the various events and the number of would-be spectators continued to grow each year. The number of entries which can be accepted in any one year is, of course, regulated by the number of matches which can be played on the courts available during the fortnight. The numbers of spectators are limited only by the accommodation available. Wimbledon will only hold about 30,000 people, and there has to be an annual ballot for seats. I believe that if, by a stroke of the pen, the accommodation could be doubled there would still be many would-be spectators who could not get a seat—or even standing room.

Lieut.-Colonel Duncan Macaulay continued to act as secretary to the All-England Club and became an ambassador of British lawn tennis overseas, representing the Club on the Continent, in the United States, and even as far afield as Australia. It is difficult to over-estimate the great power for good he exercised in the world of lawn tennis generally.

The new Lawn Tennis Association secretary, Mr. S. B. Reay, was also taking a prominent place as Britain's lawn tennis representative, and the world game owes much to Mr. J. Eaton Griffith, C.M.G., O.B.E., Britain's representative in the International Lawn Tennis Federation.

Captain A. K. Trower, who had been appointed referee of the championships after the war, died in 1950, and his place was taken in 1951 by his assistant, Colonel W. J. Legg, O.B.E.

The Wimbledon Championships are controlled by a strong

committee from the All-England Club and the Lawn Tennis Association with that very popular personality, Group Captain Sir Louis Greig, K.B.E., C.V.O., D.L., as chairman. The smooth running of the championships owed much to Sir Louis's charming personality and indefatigable hard work.

But although Wimbledon has remained the centre of British lawn tennis—and indeed the Mecca of lawn tennis players all over the world—it is in the clubs, the county associations, the services, the public parks and the schools that its roots are spreading and its popularity growing. The British Lawn Tennis Association is taking energetic and long-term steps to encourage and train young players, but the fact remains that the first seven years of lawn tennis after the Second World War were a very lean period indeed for Britain. And this applied particularly to the men, as we did generally manage to have one or two of our leading women included in the world's first ten. The only man of world class we could produce in this period was Tony Mottram. He indeed put up some wonderful performances against the world's best, but he never could produce that little bit of steel in his mentality to give us hope that he might see a whole world championship through to victory. Nevertheless he and the gallant and always reliable Geoffrey Paish deserved well of Britain in the post-war period.

On the women's side we were better served; but the women's scene was, of course, completely dominated by the Americans.

In Mrs. Jean Bostock we had a perfectly built natural athlete who, despite the fact that she lacked a big service and was unable for family reasons to take the game half as seriously as the Americans, yet was a match for their best. Had she been able to give any one of the first four years after the war to intensive practice and tournament play, I believe she had every chance of beating any other woman in the world.

Mrs. Kay Menzies, the only other British woman player of class after the war was, of course, nearing her best just before the war started. But even after her six-year lay-off she was, after Mrs. Bostock, the player the Americans feared most. Mrs. Walker-Smith, Mrs. Hilton, Miss Joan Curry (who actually beat the great Miss Brough in the French hard court championships), Mrs. Blair (in doubles), Mrs. Rinkel-Quertier, Mrs. Mottram, Miss Tuckey and Miss Partridge were all potential threats to the leading Americans without being actual menaces. Like Tony Mottram they put up good performances but could never quite get the important set in the important match, which is the quality which separates the champion from the good player.

These are my leading world players on all surfaces between 1946 and 1952, both inclusive.

MEN'S SINGLES

1.	J. A. Kramer	U.S.A.	6.	R. Savitt	U.S.A.
2.	F. A. Sedgman	Australia	7.	B. Patty	U.S.A.
3.	R. A. Gonzales	U.S.A.	8.	V. Seixas	U.S.A.
4.	F. R. Schroeder	U.S.A.	9.	H. Flam	U.S.A.
5.	J. Drobny	Egypt	10.	K. McGregor	Australia

MEN'S DOUBLES

1.	Sedgman and McGregor	Australia
2.	Sedgman and Bromwich	Australia
3.	Quist and Bromwich	Australia
4.	Kramer and Schroeder	U.S.A.
5.	Mulloy and Talbert	U.S.A.
6.	Sidwell and Bromwich	Australia
7.	Gonzales and Parker	U.S.A.
8.	T. Brown and Kramer	U.S.A.
9.	Mervyn Rose and V. Seixas	Australia and U.S.A.
10.	Drobny and Sturgess	Egypt and South Africa

LADIES' SINGLES

1.	Miss Pauline Betz	U.S.A.	6. Mrs. Jean Bostock	Great Britain
2.	Miss Louise Brough	U.S.A.	7. Mrs. Pat Todd	U.S.A.
3.	Mrs. Margaret du Pont	U.S.A.	8. Miss Shirley Fry	U.S.A.
4.	Miss Doris Hart	U.S.A.	9. Mrs. Nancye Bolton	Australia
5.	Miss Maureen Connolly	U.S.A.	10. Mrs. Chaffee-Kiner	U.S.A.

WOMEN'S DOUBLES

1. Miss Brough and Mrs. du Pont	U.S.A.
2. Mrs. Todd and Miss Hart	U.S.A.
3. Miss Hart and Miss Fry	U.S.A.
4. Mrs. Bostock and Mrs. Blair	Great Britain
5. Mrs. Todd and Miss Moran	U.S.A.
6. Mrs. Bostock and Mrs. Hilton	Great Britain
7. Mrs. Menzies and Mrs. Blair	Great Britain
8. Mrs. Menzies and Mrs. Bostock	Great Britain

MIXED DOUBLES

1. F. Sedgman and Miss Hart
2. J. Bromwich and Miss Brough
3. W. Talbert and Mrs. du Pont
4. E. Sturgess and Miss Brough
5. K. McGregor and Mrs. du Pont
6. T. Brown and Miss Brough
7. E. Sturgess and Mrs. Summers
8. Mervyn Rose and Mrs. Bolton
9. G. Brown and Mrs. Todd
10. J. Drobny and Mrs. Todd

Chapter Five

THE DAVIS CUP

T HE DAVIS CUP COMPETITION was started in 1900
when the Cup was presented by Mr. Dwight Davis, then
one of America's leading players. It was intended as an
annual international competition for men of all nations, the
contest consisting of four singles and a double, but with only
two men allowed to play the four singles. On the first day
the two singles choices played one another, on the second
day the doubles match was played, and on the third day the
two singles exponents played in the reverse order the opponent they had not played on the first day. Thus a team could
consist of only two players, or it could consist of four—the
two singles players and an entirely separate doubles pair.

From small beginnings the Davis Cup became the greatest
international athletic contest in the world of sport, with
as many as thirty-three nations challenging in one year.
Although so many nations have challenged for the Cup each
year, only four have ever won it—America, the British Isles
(including Ireland), Australasia (and Australia) and France—
Australasia being the earlier combination of Australia and
New Zealand.

In the initial year 1900 the British Isles were the only
challengers, and they sent over a team of three players—
A. W. Gore, who won the Wimbledon singles in 1899 and
1901; E. D. Black; and H. Roper Barrett, one of the brainiest
players in singles or doubles ever to set foot on a court. The
United States also relied on three players—M. D. Whitman,
the reigning singles champion; Dwight Davis, the donor of
the Cup, who had twice been runner-up in the All-comers
American Championships; and H. Ward, the 1904 American
champion. The match was played at Longwood, Boston,

U.S.A., on August 8th, 9th and 10th, and was won fairly easily by the United States.

There was no challenge in 1901, and then in 1902 the British Isles challenged again with a strong team which included J. Pim, the 1893–94 Wimbledon champion, and the famous brothers Doherty. For America W. A. Larned took the place of Davis. The match was again played at Boston and resulted in a close struggle, with America the victors by three matches to two.

In 1903 the British Isles challenged again with a two-man team consisting of the Doherty brothers—and they were successful in bringing the Cup back to Britain where it was to remain until 1907.

In 1904 the field had widened with challenges coming from Belgium, France and Austria. Austria retired and Belgium beat France. The challenge round was played at Wimbledon in July, and the British Isles team, consisting of the two Dohertys and F. L. Riseley, who won both his singles, were victorious by five matches to love.

The next year America returned to the fray, with France, Belgium, Austria and Australasia. America beat France; and Australasia, represented by that famous couple, Norman Brookes and Anthony Wilding, together with A. W. Dunlop, came through to the final. Wilding, then twenty-one years of age, was an undergraduate at Cambridge University and had never met Brookes before. But they found the Americans, represented by B. C. Wright, W. A. Larned and H. Ward, too strong for them and failed to win a single match. The challenge round, played at Wimbledon in July, was a great triumph for the British Isles, who won by five matches to love, although three of the matches went the full five sets. H. L. Doherty, "Little Do", beat both Ward and Larned in five sets, and S. H. Smith of the pulverising forehand drive only took four sets to win each of his singles. The Doherty brothers, however, who were just ending their long reign at Wimbledon, only managed to subdue the powerful volleying attack of Ward and Beals Wright at 8–6 in the fifth set of a long and exhausting match.

In 1906 the challenge round of the Davis Cup, between America and the British Isles, was played at Wimbledon

47 The Davis Cup doubles of 1952. Tony Trabert and Ted Schroeder (U.S.A.) (*in the foreground*) lose to the great Australian pair, Frank Sedgman and Ken McGregor

48   The British team of 1934. *From left to right:* H. G. N. Lee; F. J. Perry; H. W. Austin; G. P. Hughes; with non-playing Captain, H. Roper Barrett

49   Australia, 1950. *From left to right:* G. Worthington; K. McGregor; F. A. Sedgman; H. Hopman (Captain) and J. Bromwich

before the championships, and Britain relied on the same team as the year before. Once again the smashing forehand drive of S. H. Smith gained him two easy singles victories in straight sets against H. Ward and R. D. Little, but H. L. Doherty only managed to beat Little in five sets. The brothers Doherty beat Ward and Little in five sets, and Britain had again resisted the challenge by five matches to love.

In the Wimbledon Championships of that year H. L. Doherty retained his singles title for the fifth and last time, but in the doubles S. H. Smith and F. L. Riseley repeated their 1902 victory over the famous brothers. It was their swan-song in big tennis, and with the simultaneous retirement of Smith and Riseley a golden era in British lawn tennis came to an end.

For the 1907 Wimbledon Championships Norman Brookes came over from Australia in greater form than ever. But, after a hard victory over his team-mate, Anthony Wilding, he had the greatest difficulty in subduing the dynamic volleying attack of a young American student, Karl Behr. Brookes eventually won the Wimbledon title, and, with Wilding, overcame the Americans, Behr and Beals Wright, in the doubles.

In the Davis Cup match between Australasia and America, however, which took place at Wimbledon a fortnight later, the American pair turned the tables in the doubles, but Australasia came through a very close tie by three matches to two. For the challenge round Australasia relied again on her two-man team of Brookes and Wilding, whilst the British Isles also put into the lists a two-man team of A. W. Gore and Roper Barrett, who had been her representatives in the first ever Davis Cup match in 1900. And what a gallant defence these two British veterans put up! On the first day Brookes beat Gore in straight sets, and Wilding beat Barrett. On the second day, when Australasia led in the doubles by two sets and had reached 5–3 and match point in the third, the Cup looked as good as lost. But the British Isles pair had other ideas. They bravely staved off defeat, won the set and the next, and eventually won the match at 13–11 in the final set. What a pair! Then Gore proceeded to win his single against Wilding. But Norman Brookes was in crushing form against Roper Barrett, and the Cup departed to Australia where it was to remain for five years.

In 1908 the British Isles and America were the only two challengers. They played their match in Boston in September, Britain being represented by a two-man team of M. J. G. Ritchie and the Irishman, J. C. Parke. Ritchie did well to beat Beals Wright in straight sets, but that was the only match the British Isles won. The American champion, W. A. Larned, was in his second year of five American singles titles running and was too strong for both our players. F. B. Alexander and H. H. Hackett won the doubles for America, and we lost the tie by four matches to one.

For the challenge round, played in Melbourne in November, both countries relied on two-men teams—and a very close contest resulted. Brookes and Wilding had trained thoroughly for this match—Brookes being very difficult in this respect as he was easily over-trained. Alexander took him to five sets before succumbing, and Beals Wright, by clever drop shots and lobs, drained Wilding's resources and beat him in four sets as he had done in the previous year. Australasia won the doubles by the narrowest margin, after five fierce sets. Wright then covered himself with glory by defeating Norman Brookes at 12–10 in the fifth set to square the contest at two matches all. On an intensely hot day both men were utterly exhausted at the finish. But Wilding, always cool in an emergency, beat Alexander easily in the final match.

The 1909 preliminaries followed much the same course as the year before. The American champion, W. A. Larned, then at the height of his form, was too good for Britain's two singles players, C. P. Dixon and J. C. Parke, as was W. J. Clothier, the American second string; and the British pair just lost the doubles to H. H. Hackett and R. D. Little.

The challenge round was played at Sydney in November. Brookes and Wilding were too strong for the American challengers, young M. E. McLoughlin and M. H. Long, and won all five matches. But the holders had it by no means all their own way in the doubles.

There was no contest in 1910, and in 1911 the British Isles and America had to play off for the right to challenge

Australasia. Our team of C. P. Dixon, A. H. Lowe and A. E. Beamish could only win one match, the doubles, in which Dixon and Beamish beat R. D. Little and T. C. Bundy with considerable ease. Dixon indeed did very well to take Larned to a close fifth-set single.

Once more, however, the Australasians staved off the challenge by five matches to love, though they were without the services of the Wimbledon champion, A. F. Wilding.

In 1912 France re-entered the competition and played the British Isles at Folkestone in July. The British Isles team of C. P. Dixon, A. W. Gore and H. Roper Barrett, won by four matches to one, and, with America dropping out, Britain had the right to challenge Australasia. The British Isles selections were C. P. Dixon, J. C. Parke and A. E. Beamish. Australasia were again without the services of Wilding and they played Brookes and R. W. Heath in the singles and Brookes and A. W. Dunlop in the doubles.

J. C. Parke electrified everyone in the opening match by beating Norman Brookes in four sets. Parke was an Irish Rugby international and he moved about a lawn tennis court at express speed, often getting back almost hopeless shots for complete winners. Although never quite consistent enough to win championships, he could put up the most amazing performances—which he certainly did on this occasion. Dixon beat Heath in four sets, and Parke and Beamish easily beat Brookes and Dunlop in the double. Brookes beat Dixon in straight sets to square the match, but Parke easily beat Heath—and the Cup was back in Britain again.

Nineteen thirteen saw the first big expansion in the Davis Cup entry—America, Australasia, Canada, South Africa, Belgium, France and Germany all challenging the British Isles. Germany's début was singularly successful. At Wiesbaden on June 3rd, 4th and 5th, she beat France by four matches to one. A. H. Gobert, the French champion of 1911, could only get one set against O. Kreuzer, who did not win the German championship until 1920. The only French win was that of M. Decugis, the French champion, who beat F. W. Rahe.

America and Australasia met in New York, the former winning by four matches to one. Maurice McLoughlin, the reigning American champion, who was to deliver such a strong challenge to Wilding at Wimbledon, was a dynamic personality and a destructive player with his tremendous service and intensive volleying attack. He was altogether too overwhelming for Stanley Doust and H. Rice, the two Australasian singles players. R. N. Williams, who succeeded McLoughlin as American champion, was also a fine player and won both his singles, though with considerably greater difficulty. S. N. Doust and A. B. Jones, however, won the doubles for Australasia, beating McLoughlin and Hackett at 9–7 in the fifth set. This was a fine effort on the part of the Australasian pair, but Doust was one of the cleverest doubles players in the world, and Jones was outstanding in this match.

The tie between Canada and South Africa was played at Queen's Club, London, just before the Wimbledon Championships, and was won by Canada by four matches to one.

In the second round America beat Germany at Nottingham in July by five matches to love. America played the same team as before, Germany being represented by O. Kreuzer and O. Froitzheim in the singles and F. W. Rahe and H. Kleinschroth in the doubles.

Canada beat Belgium by four matches to love at Folkestone, but were not good enough to extend the strong American team in the final round.

And so the stage was set for the challenge round between America and the British Isles, which was played at Wimbledon on July 25th, 26th and 28th. Once again J. C. Parke gave the British Isles a magnificent start by beating McLoughlin in a tense five-setter, which was in doubt to the very end. Williams, however, levelled matters by winning just as close a match against that very clever and artistic British player, C. P. Dixon. For the doubles match the British Isles played Roper Barrett and Dixon, who, only three weeks before, had covered themselves with glory by winning the men's doubles at Wimbledon for the second year running. There was much speculation as to how the finesse of the two clever British Isles players would stand up to the thunderbolts of McLoughlin. In a breathlessly exciting match the British Isles actually came within a stroke of victory, but in the end the crushing power of McLoughlin was too much for them. Just that one point would have decided the match, as J. C. Parke overcame R. N. Williams in another of his non-stop all-out Rugby football sort of matches. I am not suggesting for a moment that J. C. Parke was not a very fine lawn tennis player; he certainly was, and he proved it once again seven years later when he turned back the challenge at Wimbledon of the American champion, W. M. Johnston. But it was Parke's tremendous speed about the court, his *élan*, and his never-say-die spirit which brought him so many unexpected victories over the world's greatest players. Parke was always a good man to have on your side, either at lawn tennis or Rugby football.

In 1914 the competing nations were the same as before, except that South Africa dropped out. The British Isles, playing Parke and T. Mavrogordato in the singles, and Roper Barrett and Mavrogordato in the doubles, beat Belgium at Folkestone in July by five matches to love.

Australasia, playing their old two-man team of Brookes and Wilding, beat Canada all ends up at Chicago.

Germany and France had byes.

In the second round the British Isles beat France at Wimbledon by four matches to one. Parke and "Mavro" each won their singles for the British Isles against Decugis and M. Germot, but the British pair of "Mavro" and Roper Barrett lost to the Frenchmen in the double.

Australasia, playing the same two-man team of Brookes and Wilding, beat Germany at Pittsburg, U.S.A., by five matches to love, at the end of July almost as the war was starting. The atmosphere in which this match was played was certainly rather extraordinary; war clouds were thickening daily, and the German players, who were both in the Army Reserve, had to consult their Consul before taking the court. At Wimbledon Brookes had only just managed to beat Froitzheim at 8–6 in the fifth set, but Brookes's always rather delicate physique had been strained by a fortnight's play in exceptional heat. At Chicago, however, fit and fresh, Brookes defeated both Froitzheim and Kreuzer in straight sets—as did Wilding. The two Australians, fresh from their triumph in the doubles at Wimbledon, were much too strong for the German pair. The German players never reached the

Fatherland. Their boat was intercepted by a British warship, and they spent the war as prisoners in Britain.

The final round between Australasia and the British Isles was played at Boston on August 6th, 7th and 8th—and they had to hurry as the war was just starting. A. R. F. Kingscote, who was a regular officer in the British Army, had to leave for home before the match started. J. C. Parke played another great match against Brookes, but just failed in the fifth set to repeat his triumph of 1912 at Melbourne. A. H. Lowe, playing second single for the British Isles, went down in straight sets to Wilding, but only after having run him to 14–16 in the third. Had Lowe won this set he might easily have won the match as Wilding was quite exhausted. Brookes and Wilding slaughtered Parke and Mavrogordato in the doubles, and, with Australasia having won the match 3–0, they called it a day, and a week later the challenge round between Australasia and the United States was played in New York. And what a grand finale it was! The atmosphere was just like a Turkish bath, as it can be in New York at that time of the year.

On the first day the gallant red-head, Maurice McLoughlin, beat Norman Brookes 17–15, 6–3, 6–3. The first tremendous set killed Brookes, now over thirty and never blessed with tremendous stamina. Wilding, however, beat Williams very easily. In the doubles Brookes and Wilding, the Wimbledon doubles champions, beat McLoughlin and T. C. Bundy, the American doubles champions, 6–3, 8–6, 9–7. This really decided the contest as Brookes could hardly lose to Williams, and he beat him easily in the first match on the third day. In the last match McLoughlin gained a magnificent victory over Wilding by three sets to one, thus reversing the result of their great encounter at Wimbledon in 1913—but it cannot be said that Wilding was playing with his previous power and concentration. The approach of war weighed heavily on his mind.

This match marked the end of an epoch both in the history of the Davis Cup and in the world of lawn tennis generally. Anthony Wilding, then only just thirty, never played again and was killed in France the next year. Brookes, then aged thirty-seven, played again after the war—and, indeed, played brilliantly—but was, of course, by that time long past his best. The "Californian comet", Maurice McLoughlin, lost his singles title to Williams in the American championship of that year, retained his doubles title with Bundy, and then never appeared again on the champions' roll or in Davis Cup tennis. He was on overseas service during the war, and when he did return to the tennis scene he was but a shadow of his former self. R. N. Williams, still only a comparative youngster, won the American championship in 1914 and again in 1916 and played Davis Cup doubles for America after the war. Bundy won the American doubles with McLoughlin for the third time running in 1914, and then did not appear again on the championship roll.

For the next five years there was no Davis Cup competition, and, except in America, tournament and championship lawn tennis closed down in most countries of the world. The Davis Cup was won by Australasia for the sixth time—the British Isles having won it five times and America four.

When the war was over, the Davis Cup competition got under way slowly and in 1919 only four nations challenged Australasia—France, Belgium, the British Isles and South Africa. France and Belgium met at Brussels in July, M. Decugis again turning out for France and winning the singles and double in which he played. When France had won the first three matches the remainder of the tie was called off.

The British Isles beat South Africa at Eastbourne in August by four matches to one. A. R. F. Kingscote, who had come through to the final of the All-comers at the first post-war Wimbledon, before he was hardly out of uniform, played first single for Britain and beat both G. H. Dodd and the left-hander, L. Raymond. Mavrogordato, the second singles player, who could still run farther and faster than most on a tennis court, won one of his singles, and Roper Barrett and Kingscote won the double in straight sets.

The British Isles and France fought out the final round at Deauville in September, and Britain won a close contest by three matches to two. Kingscote and Roper Barrett were chosen again for the British Isles, but Mavrogordato gave way to P. M. Davson, the British covered court champion, for the second singles place, and O. G. N. Turnbull partnered

Roper Barrett in the double instead of Kingscote. France relied on a two-man team of A. H. Gobert and W. H. Laurentz. Kingscote again won both his singles matches, but Davson lost to Gobert and only just managed to beat Laurentz. With Barrett and Turnbull losing in straight sets it was indeed a close call for the British Isles.

This meant, of course, making the long journey to Australia for the challenge round, which was staged at Sydney in January. A trip to Australia was a very different business in those days from what it became thirty years later. In 1919 it was a long sea voyage each way—in 1949 it was a matter of four days in an aeroplane. Perhaps that is why lawn tennis players lived longer (in the championship ranks) in the days of restful sea voyages. The modern champion would have probably competed in a couple of tournaments whilst the oldster was still on the boat.

Australasia were able to rely on two young post-war players for the singles, G. L. Patterson, the reigning Wimbledon champion, and J. O. Anderson, who was to win the Australian championship in 1922, 1924 and 1925. Patterson was chosen to partner the veteran, Norman Brookes, in the double. The British Isles sent Kingscote and A. H. Lowe for the singles, and A. E. Beamish to partner Kingscote in the double. Patterson was too good for both his singles opponents. Kingscote beat Anderson comfortably, and Lowe went very near indeed to doing so. But Brookes and Patterson crushed the British Isles doubles pair for the loss of only two games. So for the first year after the war the Cup remained in Australasia.

In 1920 the number of challengers was five, including a newcomer in the Netherlands. The others were America, France, South Africa and the British Isles. The Netherlands beat South Africa by three matches to two, and then, in the second match of the series between the United States and France, played at Eastbourne in July, the famous new American players made their first appearance in the Davis Cup. W. T. "Big Bill" Tilden had just won the Wimbledon championship singles title at his first attempt, and W. M. "Little Bill" Johnston was the reigning American champion. They formed a formidable two-man team and overcame

Gobert and Laurentz of France in the two singles and doubles matches played.

In the second round, played a week later at Wimbledon, the same two-man American team beat a British Isles two-man team of Kingscote and Parke by five matches to love. But the Americans didn't have things all their own way by any means. Johnston reversed his Wimbledon defeat by Parke a fortnight before but lost two sets in the process. He had an even closer call against Kingscote and only came through at 7–5 in the fifth set. The Americans also lost two sets in winning the doubles, but Tilden won both his singles without very great difficulty.

The challenge round between the United States and Australasia was played at Auckland, New Zealand, at the end of December. The Americans again relied on a two-man team of Tilden and Johnston, and Australasia also relied on a two-man team of Brookes and Patterson. Brookes, now aged forty-three, was attempting to give Tilden sixteen years in age, but he took a set from both Tilden and Johnston and proved that he must still be ranked amongst the world's greatest players. Patterson took a set from Tilden but was massacred by Johnston who only allowed him five games. Johnston, who was a small man of slight but wiry physique, always revelled in speed and was particularly severe on Patterson's big service, which he slammed for outright winners. And so the Davis Cup returned home to the United States where it was destined to remain until 1927.

In 1921 the competition for the Cup started to spread itself wider amongst the lawn tennis playing nations. Japan, India, Denmark, Argentina, Czechoslavakia and Spain entered the lists for the first time, and altogether ten nations challenged the United States. In the first round Argentina and Denmark had byes, and the British Isles played Spain at Hendon in the first match towards the end of May. The British team was an entirely new one. F. G. Lowe, brother of A. H. Lowe, played with Randolph Lycett in the singles, and Lycett and Woosnam, who were to win the Wimbledon doubles that year, were paired for the double. Lycett was one of the best doubles players in the world, winning the Wimbledon doubles three years running with different partners. Lowe beat Count de Gomar, but had not quite got the guns to cope with that lovely stylist, Manuel Alonso, who was ranked that year Number 8 in the world. Lycett did exceedingly well to win both his singles, and he and Woosnam made certain of the double; so that the British Isles were through by four matches to one.

Australasia beat Canada 5–0, and Belgium beat Czechoslovakia.

In the next round the British Isles, playing Max Woosnam and F. G. Lowe in the singles and Woosnam and Turnbull in the double, just went down to Australasia at Pittsburg, U.S.A., by the odd match. Denmark and Japan had byes; Belgium and Argentina retired.

India and France met in Paris in July when India gained a meritorious victory by four matches to one. The amazing Mahomet Sleem, waging his usual clever war of attrition, won both his singles against the French champion, J. Samazeuilh, and W. H. Laurentz. S. M. Jacob lost to Samazeuilh, and with L. S. Deane, whom I partnered once in the Indian championships, just managed to beat Laurentz and Brugnon in the double.

Australasia beat Denmark by five matches to love, and Japan, having received two walk-overs, played their first ever Davis Cup match against India at Chicago, U.S.A., in August. Japan had two first-rate players in Z. Shimizu, ranked that year as high as Number 4 in the world, and K. Kumagae, and won by five matches to love. And this strong Japanese two-man team went on to beat Australia at Newport, U.S.A., by four matches to one.

The challenge round between the U.S.A. and Japan, played in New York in September, was won by the United States by five matches to love—but the tenacious Shimizu took the great Tilden to a fifth set before he acknowledged defeat. Once again W. M. Johnston played the second single for the U.S.A., but this time R. N. Williams and W. M. Washburn played the double for America.

Fourteen nations entered in 1922, but Canada, Hawaii, Japan and the Philippines withdrew. Australasia beat Belgium at Scarborough by four matches to love, and India won every match against Roumania. The second round match between France and Denmark, which was played at Copenhagen in June, was remarkable for the entry into Davis Cup tennis of two more of the famous "Four Musketeers" of France who were eventually to bring world tennis supremacy to their country. Jacques Brugnon had already made his début the year before, and now Jean Borotra and Henri Cochet made their bow. The fourth musketeer, René Lacoste, did not make his appearance in Davis Cup tennis until the following year. Jean Borotra won both his singles, and the doubles match in partnership with Cochet. The latter played as substitute for J. Couitéas after the tie was won and emerged victorious.

The British Isles, playing Kingscote and F. G. Lowe in singles, and Kingscote and the evergreen Frank Riseley in doubles, beat Italy at Roehampton in June in all the four matches played.

The British Isles then retired, leaving Australasia to play France in the third round at Boston, U.S.A., in August. Australasia, with G. L. Patterson and Pat O'Hara Wood, won by four matches to one, but that one match was a good five-set win by Cochet, ranked this year as Number 6 in the world, over O'Hara Wood, who was ranked seventh.

Australasia went on to beat Spain by the same margin in the final round.

The challenge round was played at Forest Hills, New York, in September, and was won by the United States by four matches to one. Tilden, who was now American champion for the third year running and at the height of his form, beat Patterson in straight sets, but had to play all five to beat Anderson. "Little Bill" Johnston, however, made mincemeat of the two Australasian speed merchants, losing only six games to Anderson and five to Patterson. What a wonderful player this little American was! Yet year after year he just couldn't beat Tilden for the American singles title.

But Tilden and Vincent Richards, the American doubles champions, had a severe trouncing in the doubles by Patterson and O'Hara Wood, only managing to get seven games in the three sets played.

In 1923, as a result of the continued expansion of the competition, certain alterations had to be made in the rules. A system of zoning was introduced; in future there were two zones, European and American, with an inter-zone final to decide who should challenge the holders. And in this year Ireland went out of the British Isles team and became a separate challenger. The Australasian nomenclature also disappeared—New Zealand and Australia challenging on their own. A record number of sixteen nations played off for the right to challenge the United States.

In the European zone, Czechoslovakia beat Switzerland by three matches to two; Ireland beat India at Dublin by three matches to two; and France beat Denmark at Bordeaux by four matches to one, Cochet and Lacoste playing the singles for France. Great Britain beat Belgium in Brussels by three matches to two. J. Washer beat both the British singles players, R. Lycett and J. B. Gilbert, but the new doubles combination of Lycett and L. A. Godfree, who were to win the Wimbledon doubles that year, trounced the Belgian pair, Washer and Watson, in the double.

In the second round of the European zone, Switzerland beat Argentina, and France beat Ireland by four matches to one. All four of the famous "Musketeers"—Cochet, Borotra, Lacoste and Brugnon—were included in the French team for the first time. Spain beat Britain at Manchester by three matches to two. J. D. P. Wheatley made his first appearance in the singles for Britain. He won a terrific five-setter against E. Flaquer, whom Lycett also beat for the loss of only two games. But Count de Gomar beat both our singles players, and Lycett and Godfree could only get one set off the Spaniards in the doubles match.

Holland gained a sweeping victory over Italy on their own courts at Noordwijk.

In the third round France beat Switzerland, and Spain were much too good for Holland.

The final of the European zone, between France and Spain, which was played at Deauville in July, was a very close affair indeed, and was won by France by three matches to two. Lacoste and P. Blanchy, the French champion, played the singles for France, and Cochet and Brugnon the double. Spain relied again on the two-man team of Count de Gomar and Flaquer. Lacoste won both his singles; Blanchy lost to

Count de Gomar but beat Flaquer, and the Spanish pair beat Cochet and Brugnon 6–4, 8–6, 11–13, 1–6, 6–4—a really terrific match.

So France became the winners of the first European zone competition.

In the American zone, Japan beat Canada 5–0, and Australia beat Hawaii 4–0.

In the final round of this zone, Australia beat Japan by 4–1.

The first inter-zone round between Australia and France was played at Boston in August and was won by Australia by four matches to one. J. O. Anderson was too severe off the ground for the French singles players, J. B. Hawkes beat Brugnon, and Anderson and Hawkes beat Brugnon and Lacoste, the French doubles choice, 6–8, 6–3, 6–3, 6–8, 9–7.

But the writing was on the wall; these young French musketeers were gaining their experience the hard way, and in a few years' time they were destined to beat the world.

In the challenge round, played at Forest Hills, New York, at the end of August and early September, the United States beat Australia by four matches to one. The Australians stuck to their winning two-man team of Anderson and Hawkes, and America played Tilden and Johnston as usual in the singles and Tilden and Williams in the double. The only match won by Australia was that in which Anderson beat Johnston in five sets—the first match Johnston had ever lost in the Davis Cup.

America won the doubles match 17–15, 11–13, 2–6, 6–3, 6–2. These Davis Cup doubles were certainly terrific.

The year 1924 was to see the start of a great period of French dominance in the lawn tennis world. Jean Borotra won at Wimbledon and one of the "Four Musketeers" won there every year for the next six years. And that dominance was to extend to Forest Hills and to the Davis Cup competition—but it had not done so yet. For two more years Tilden was to triumph at Forest Hills before the Frenchmen caught up on him, and for three more years America was to hold the Davis Cup.

In 1924 there were no less than twenty-one challengers—fifteen in the European zone and the remainder in the American. Great Britain played Belgium in the first match in the series at Torquay in May and won by three matches to two. Once more A. R. F. Kingscote led the British attack, ten years since he had first been chosen for Britain. J. B. Gilbert was the other singles player, and Max Woosnam and L. A. Godfree were the British doubles pair. The powerful left-hander, J. Washer, was too much for Kingscote, and also beat Gilbert, though only at 8–6 in the final set. Britain, however, won the other three matches without losing a set. In the second round Britain beat Spain at Birmingham in May by three matches to two. J. D. P. Wheatley replaced Kingscote in the singles, though the British team was otherwise unchanged. Spain relied on a two-man team of M. Alonso and E. Flaquer. Alonso was still ranked in the world's first ten, and, at the previous Wimbledon, Flaquer, in partnership with Count de Gomar, had overcome Borotra and Lacoste to reach the final. If Flaquer and de Gomar could have played the doubles match for their country at Birmingham it might just have turned the scale for Spain. As it was, Spain could only win M. Alonso's two singles.

In the third round Britain overcame South Africa at Scarborough in June by four matches to one. Britain played the same team which had been victorious against Spain.

In the fourth round, however, Britain met France at Eastbourne at the end of July and went down one to four. For this match Kingscote, who had been in fine form at Wimbledon and had reached the last eight, replaced Wheatley in the singles for Britain. France played H. Cochet and R. Lacoste in the singles and Borotra and Brugnon for the doubles. What a team! All four musketeers in full force. Lacoste, Borotra and Cochet were all ranked in the world's first ten, and they could afford to leave Borotra, the Wimbledon singles champion, out of the singles altogether. In these circumstances I do think the British team put up a really magnificent performance. Kingscote, giving the young Frenchmen many years in age, took them both to five sets—a really grand effort—and J. B. Gilbert did wonders to beat Cochet in a close five-set match.

The final round of the European zone, between France and Czechoslovakia, was won easily by France in August at Evian-les-Bains.

In the first round of the American zone, Canada just beat
Cuba by three matches to two, and Australia was much too
strong for China. In the final round the Australian two-man
team of G. L. Patterson and P. O'Hara Wood easily beat
Japan, and then, in the inter-zone round, beat France at
Boston by three matches to two. France left out Cochet
altogether for this match and played Lacoste in partnership
with that doyen of doubles players, "Toto" Brugnon. Although
Lacoste did win the Wimbledon doubles with Borotra in 1925
I never thought he was quite the force in doubles the other
three musketeers were, and this doubles pairing at Boston
may well have been important, as Patterson and O'Hara
Wood won the decisive double very easily. France gained
an early lead when twenty-year-old René Lacoste beat
Patterson in three sets. But O'Hara Wood, after losing two
of the first three sets, wore Borotra down to win in the fifth
set. Borotra seldom lost when he could get himself into such
a winning position at the start. The doubles went easily to
Australia, who then led 2–1, and Patterson decided the
issue by beating Borotra overwhelmingly for the loss of
only seven games.

The challenge round was played at Philadelphia in September and was won by the United States by five matches to love.
For the first time since the United States won back the Davis
Cup from Australia in 1920 "Little Bill" Johnston did not
play the second single for his country. His place as second
singles player was taken by Vincent Richards. Australia
played the same two-man team of Patterson and O'Hara
Wood; but neither of the Australians could extend either
Tilden or Vincent Richards, and the only set they got was the
first one in the double, in which the United States were
represented once again by Tilden and Johnston. It is not
always realised what a strong combination the two "Bills"
made. They are apt to be regarded as purely singles players,
but, in the 1920 challenge round, they beat Norman Brookes
and Patterson for the loss of only one set, and were just as
strong a combination when they were called upon to play
this year. Curiously enough, although they both won the
American doubles with other people, they never won
together.

In 1925 the number of challengers had increased by one in the American zone. Britain played Poland in the first round at Warsaw in May with a somewhat revised team of F. G. Lowe and J. D. P. Wheatley for the singles, and Kingsley and Godfree as the doubles pair. In the second round they beat Denmark at Copenhagen, with J. B. Gilbert in the place of Lowe. In the third round, however, Britain met France at Eastbourne in July, and, somewhat naturally, found the musketeers too strong for them. Britain played yet another team of Turnbull and Crole-Rees in the singles, and Godfree and Wheatley in the doubles. France went on to beat Holland easily in the final round.

In the third round of the American zone, Japan beat Spain at Baltimore by three matches to two in a particularly exciting contest. Japan played the two-man team of T. Harada and Z. Shimizu, whilst the Spaniards played M. Alonso and E. Flaquer in the singles, and the two Alonsos in the doubles. Both M. Alonso and T. Harada were ranked in the world's first ten at the time. Harada won both his singles; Shimizu lost both his, and the Japanese just nosed out a close five-set double match, to win by three matches to two.

In the final round of the American zone, Australia played Japan at Boston in August and won by four matches to one. Harada beat Patterson but lost to J. O. Anderson, and Australia won the other matches fairly comfortably. In the inter-zone round, played at Forest Hills in September, the young French team, now going from strength to strength, beat Australia by three matches to one, and, for the first time in the history of the competition, France reached the challenge round.

France relied for the singles on Jean Borotra and René Lacoste, the Wimbledon champion of 1924 and 1925, and on Lacoste and Borotra, the reigning Wimbledon doubles champions, for the doubles. It is an enormous tribute to the Americans that they could have beaten such a team and by the overwhelming score of five matches to love. But there was a great deal more in it than the score suggests. In the first match Borotra led Tilden by two sets to one and very nearly won the match in the fourth set. Marvellous little Bill Johnston beat Lacoste for the loss of only one set and simply slaughtered Borotra. Tilden only overcame Lacoste after a terrific match, 3–6, 10–12, 8–6, 7–5, 6–2. The American team of Vincent Richards and R. N. Williams, then the reigning American champions, beat Lacoste and Borotra, the Wimbledon champions, in three straight sets.

The number of challengers still continued to increase every year, and in 1926 there were twenty-three—eighteen in the European zone and five in the American. In the first round Britain played Poland at Harrogate in May and won by five matches to love. In the third round they just beat Italy by three matches to two; and in the fourth round beat Spain by four matches to one. In the final round, however, they met the strong French team at Cabourg in July, and France was victorious in all four of the matches played. J. C. Gregory, however, much distinguished himself in the singles by taking Cochet to five sets.

Japan came through to the final of the American zone, and, in the inter-zone round, played France at Forest Hills and only went down by two matches to three. T. Harada beat both Lacoste and Cochet, and the latter was at one time in distinct danger of going down to the second Japanese singles player, T. Tawara. In the doubles the strong team of Cochet and Brugnon, reigning Wimbledon champions, won for the loss of only two games.

For the second time the United States and France met in the challenge round, played at Philadelphia in September. The United States played the same team as the year before— Tilden and Johnston for the singles, and Williams and Vincent Richards for the doubles. "Little Bill" Johnston, however, pulverised both Lacoste and Borotra with his tremendous forehand hitting, but Tilden lost in four sets to René Lacoste. R. N. Williams and Vincent Richards were again too strong for the reigning Wimbledon champions, Cochet and Brugnon, and beat them in three straight sets.

In 1927 the field had increased yet again to twenty-five challengers—twenty-one in the European zone and four in the American. Great Britain beat Sweden at Birmingham in May by four matches to one, but went down to Denmark at Harrogate in the second round.

In the inter-zone round France played Japan for the second

year running and were victorious at Boston by three matches to love, and, for the third time running, challenged the United States at Philadelphia in September. At last the young French musketeers were triumphant and took the Cup across the Channel for the first time in its history. America again relied on Tilden and Johnston for the singles, but played Tilden and Hunter, the new Wimbledon and American doubles champions, for the doubles match. For France Lacoste and Cochet played the singles, and Borotra and Brugnon the double. In the first match Lacoste beat Johnston very easily in three straight sets. This was the second match Johnston had ever lost in the Davis Cup, but the fury of his hitting had started to wear out his somewhat frail physique and he never played again for the United States. In the second match of the first day Tilden beat Cochet in four sets, but not without considerable difficulty, and he and Hunter had to play five exhausting sets in the doubles match before beating Borotra and Brugnon. This gave America the lead by two matches to one, and France had to win both singles on the final day against the redoubtable Tilden and Johnston combination to gain the Cup. They brought it off, however, for the loss of only one set, which Tilden gained from Lacoste. America had had a long innings of seven years, and now the Cup was to stay in France for the next six years.

Yet more nations came to challenge in 1928 than ever before. They numbered actually thirty-two—twenty-six in the European zone and six in the American. Britain met Argentina in the first round of the European zone, and, with J. C. Gregory and E. Higgs as her singles players, and Crole-Rees and Eames as her doubles representatives, won by four matches to one. The same team beat Finland in the second round, and Germany in the third round. But they went down to Italy in the fourth round at Felixstowe by one match to four. The strong Italian team, headed by H. L. de Morpurgo, came through to the final. In the final round of the American zone the United States beat Japan, and then beat Italy in the inter-zone round.

So once again France and the United States met in the challenge round, but this time with the positions reversed and the United States in the role of challengers. The match was played in Paris at the end of July and won by France by four matches to one. J. F. Hennessey had taken the place of W. M. Johnston in the singles, and Tilden and Hunter once again represented the United States in the doubles. But the great Bill Tilden, who had lost his American title to the French invasion three years before, turned the tables on Lacoste and beat the Wimbledon champion in a great five-set match. Cochet, however, now the holder of the American singles championship, beat Tilden in three tremendous sets, and Cochet and Borotra beat Tilden and Hunter in the doubles after a strenuous five-set match.

The number of challengers dropped slightly in 1929—there being twenty-four in the European zone and five in the American. The British team, which beat Poland at Warsaw in May by five matches to love, contained two new singles players in H. W. Austin and G. P. Hughes, though they still relied on the same doubles combination of Crole-Rees and Eames. Austin was to reach the semi-final of that year's Wimbledon and take a set off Borotra. When Britain beat South Africa at Bournemouth in the next round she was represented by Austin and J. C. Gregory for the singles, and a new doubles combination in J. C. Gregory and I. G. Collins. Playing the same team, Britain beat Hungary at Budapest in June, but went down to Germany in Berlin in July by two matches to three in the final round of the European zone. Germany won both her singles on the first day when Prenn easily beat Gregory, and Moldenhauer also beat Austin in straight sets. Gregory and Collins, however, wiped the floor with the German doubles team to keep Great Britain in the match, and Gregory put up a splendid performance by completely overwhelming Moldenhauer to square the match. The deciding singles between Prenn and Austin was a nerve-racking affair and physically and mentally Austin couldn't quite stay the course; completely exhausted and suffering from cramp he had to give up in the final set. He was well beaten by a tougher opponent although certainly not a better player.

In the inter-zone final between the United States and Germany the U.S.A. put into the field a new team. Tilden had, as his singles partner, F. T. Hunter, who for two years had been the runner-up in the American Championships.

The American doubles pair was W. Allison and J. van Ryn, the reigning Wimbledon champions and one of the most dynamic pairs ever. The United States beat Germany by five matches to love—Tilden winning both his singles with the greatest ease. And so again to yet another challenge round between France and the United States.

Played at Paris at the end of July it resulted in one of those epic international contests in which the history of the Davis Cup abounds. This year only two of the famous "Four Musketeers" were defending the Cup—Henri Cochet, the current Wimbledon champion, and Jean Borotra in the singles—René Lacoste being out of action through illness—and Cochet and Borotra in the doubles. America chose G. M. Lott to play the second singles to Tilden, and W. L. Allison and J. van Ryn, the reigning Wimbledon doubles champions, as their doubles pair. Henri Cochet, now ranked as the leading player in the world, beat the great Tilden with ridiculous ease for the loss of only six games, and also beat Lott fairly comfortably. Jean Borotra never managed to beat Tilden out of doors and could only get the first set from him, although he beat Lott in four sets. Allison and van Ryn, who were a really great doubles combination, beat Borotra and Cochet in three straight sets.

In 1930 twenty-eight nations challenged France for the Cup—twenty-four in the European zone and four in the American. Great Britain played Germany at Queen's Club, London, in April and won by three matches to two. H. W. Austin, now ranked amongst the world's first ten and a stronger player both nervously and physically, lost to H. Landmann, but beat his former conqueror, D. Prenn, in three straight sets. H. G. N. Lee, a newcomer to the Davis Cup, lost to Prenn but beat Landmann. Gregory and Collins, however, won their doubles match comfortably. In their second round match against Poland, Britain won by five matches to love, playing Nigel Sharpe as her second singles player with Harold Lee. Gregory and Collins slaughtered the Polish doubles pair without losing a single game. But in the third round Australia beat the British team by four matches to one. The single British point was won by the ever stalwart doubles pair, Gregory and Collins.

Italy beat Japan in the final round of the European zone by three matches to two.

In the inter-zone round the U.S.A. beat Italy by four matches to one.

So, for the sixth year running, France and the U.S.A. met in the challenge round. The match was played in Paris at the end of July and resulted in a win for France by four matches to one. France was without her great champion, René Lacoste, always the most frail physically of the "Four Musketeers", though possibly the greatest player of them all. He was never again to play for France. Cochet and Borotra were the singles players, and Cochet paired with Brugnon for the doubles. The veteran "Big Bill" Tilden was playing in his last challenge round for America with G. M. Lott as his second singles string. Tilden had just regained the Wimbledon singles title and was still very much a force to be reckoned with, as he proved when he beat Borotra, as he had done at Wimbledon—and indeed as he had never failed to do on any other surface than wood. But that was the only match America won. Cochet and Brugnon revenged the French doubles defeat of the year before when they beat Allison and van Ryn in straight sets.

And so to 1931 when thirty nations challenged the holders. A new grouping was introduced this year by dividing the American zone into two parts—North and South. Great Britain beat first Monaco, then Belgium and South Africa, Japan, and, in the final round, Czechoslovakia.

In the inter-zone (final) round, played in Paris in July, Great Britain beat the United States by three matches to two. The old American champions who had dominated the world of lawn tennis for so long had departed and both Britain and the U.S.A. were putting a new generation of players into the field. And so Great Britain, for the first time for twelve years, reached the challenge round, which was played in Paris at the end of July. The famous musketeers, now veterans of the world's courts, turned out as usual in all their might and glory to defend the Cup—and never did Frenchmen fight better than when they were representing their country. Henri Cochet, ranked for the last four years as premier player in the world, beat H. W. Austin, ranked that year as Number 2 in the world, in four sets. F. J. Perry, up and coming British player who had reached the semi-final at Wimbledon, beat Jean Borotra in a long five-set match to square the tie. In the doubles Cochet and Brugnon beat G. P. Hughes and C. H. Kingsley to give France the lead by two matches to one. On the third day Austin also beat Borotra, but Cochet beat Perry in four sets and the Cup was won by France for the fifth year running. Now, however, Britain was exerting greater pressure on the champions.

Again there were thirty challengers in 1932 and Britain came through to the fourth round, only to go down to Germany. D. Prenn was too tough for both Austin and Perry, and von Cramm beat Austin also—but lost to Perry. Britain's doubles pair, however, Perry and Hughes, gained an easy victory in straight sets.

Those old rivals, France and the United States, met in the challenge round in Paris, and France just held the Cup by three matches to two. The famous musketeers, never quite the same power without Lacoste, were nearing the end of their reign. H. Ellsworth Vines beat Cochet, and Allison and van Ryn beat Cochet and Brugnon in the doubles.

In 1933 there was a record number of thirty-three challengers, and for the second time in three years the ever-improving British team came through to the challenge round. In a momentous match in Paris at the end of July they ended France's long reign by three matches to two. On the first day Austin beat A. Merlin in three sets, and Perry struck the vital blow for Britain by beating Cochet in five sets. Borotra and Brugnon easily beat H. G. N. Lee and G. P. Hughes in the double, to keep the match alive. On the third day Cochet played one of his most gallant matches for his country by beating Austin in the fifth set after having been up against it all the way. It was a nerve-racking moment for Perry who had many uneasy moments before beating Merlin in the deciding match(46).

So, after twenty-two years, the Cup came back to Britain. And that grand old player and astute non-playing captain, H. Roper Barrett, must be given full credit for the part he played in Britain's victory.

In 1934 the United States came through to challenge Great

Britain at Wimbledon at the end of July(48). Britain's two singles players, F. J. Perry, the new Wimbledon champion, and H. W. Austin, were now ranked Number 1 and Number 4 in the world respectively. The American singles players, S. B. Wood and F. X. Shields, were ranked Number 6 and Number 8. The two British players won both their singles matches. G. M. Lott and L. R. Stoefen, the Wimbledon and American doubles champions, were too good for G. P. Hughes and H. G. N. Lee in the doubles.

In 1935 the challengers were again the United States, who had a completely new team. They played J. D. Budge, Wimbledon semi-finalist, and W. L. Allison, who was to win the American singles title that year, in the singles, and the old powerful combination of Allison and van Ryn, once again the reigning Wimbledon doubles holders. But the two grand British singles players, Perry and Austin, won both their matches, and a new doubles pairing of G. P. Hughes and C. R. D. Tuckey achieved a great triumph by winning the doubles match and thereby reversing the result of their doubles defeat by Allison and van Ryn at Wimbledon. The greatest credit must be given to that very clever doubles player, G. P. Hughes, who, sometimes with rather moderate partners, had kept the flag of Britain's doubles prestige flying through many years in the wilderness.

Twenty-three nations challenged in 1936, and this time Australia, who had defeated the United States by three matches to two, came through to challenge Great Britain. Perry, for the third time running, was the Wimbledon champion, and H. W. Austin had reached the semi-final. They were ranked that year Number 1 and Number 5 in the world. G. P. Hughes and C. R. D. Tuckey were the Wimbledon doubles champions. Australia put into the field J. H. Crawford, Wimbledon champion of 1933 and the world's sixth ranking player, and A. K. Quist, the reigning Australian champion and the fourth ranking player in the world. For the doubles Australia played Crawford and Quist, Wimbledon doubles champions of the preceding year. It was indeed a battle of giants! Austin gave Britain a wonderful start by beating Crawford in the first match in four sets, and Perry beat Quist by the same margin. Crawford and Quist, however, kept the match alive by winning the doubles. Then Quist played marvellously to beat Austin, and it was left to Perry to decide the issue with his great Australian rival, Jack Crawford. Perry rose to the occasion magnificently, and, in his last match for Great Britain before turning professional, he overwhelmed the Australian for the loss of only eight games.

For four years Great Britain had held the Cup against the world's best. It was a triumph of team-work, fitness, high morale and wise captaincy.

Twenty-four countries challenged for the Cup in 1937—twenty in the European zone and four in the American. Germany, led by G. von Cramm, ranked as the Number 2 player in the world, came through as the winners of the European zone. The final round of the American zone, played at New York at the end of May, was between the United States and Australia. J. D. Budge, who had succeeded Perry as the world's leading player and was to succeed him as Wimbledon champion, beat J. H. Crawford of Australia very easily, and also beat John Bromwich. The United States won by five matches to love.

The inter-zone round between the United States and Germany was played at Wimbledon at the end of July, and a really magnificent contest was won by the United States by three matches to two. America played J. D. Budge and G. M. Grant in the singles, with Budge and Mako, the Wimbledon doubles champions and the American doubles champions of 1936 and 1938, as their doubles pair. Germany played a two-man team of G. von Cramm and H. Henkel. On the first day Budge beat Henkel for the loss of only six games, and von Cramm beat Grant just as easily. America's fine doubles team won the doubles match on the second day in four close sets, and on the third day Henkel levelled the scores by beating Grant in four sets. The fifth and deciding match was one of the most thrilling in the whole history of the Davis Cup. Budge lost the first two sets and was trailing 1–4 in the final set, but just managed to pull it out at 8–6, which was one of his very finest performances.

The challenge round between the U.S.A. and Great Britain took place at Wimbledon a few days later. Britain played C. E. Hare with Austin in the singles in place of F. J. Perry, and C. R. D. Tuckey and F. H. D. Wilde in the doubles. The Americans replaced Grant by F. A. Parker in the singles—otherwise their team was the same as for the inter-zone round. Austin played splendidly to beat Parker in the first match in three sets, and Budge had to play a long 15–13 first set against Hare, who had then given all he could. Budge and Mako put the U.S.A. ahead by winning a stiff four-set double, and on the third day Great Britain lost the Davis Cup when Parker easily beat Hare in the first match. And so for the first time for ten years the Davis Cup returned to its original home in the United States.

There were twenty-five challengers in 1938, and Britain once more had to plough her way through the preliminary rounds. She just beat Roumania by three matches to two in the first round, but went down heavily to Jugoslavia in the second round. Britain was now playing a completely new team of R. A. Shayes and D. W. Butler in the singles and Butler and Wilde in the doubles. The final round of the European zone between Germany and Yugoslavia was played at Berlin at the end of July, and Germany, without their leading player, von Cramm, only came through by three matches to two. Australia came through the American zone and beat Germany very easily in the inter-zone round.

The challenge round between the United States and Australia was played at Philadelphia in September and won by the United States by three matches to two. The American team was slightly changed from the year before with R. L. Riggs playing second singles to Budge, instead of F. A. Parker. Budge, the Wimbledon champion and leading player in the world, was making his last appearance in the Davis Cup as he had decided, like Perry two years before, to turn professional. The Australians played a two-man team of John Bromwich and A. K. Quist. On the first day Riggs beat Quist and Budge beat Bromwich, to give the United States a winning lead. On the second day the magnificent Australian doubles pair of Bromwich and Quist, certainly one of the best in the history of the game, beat the Americans in four sets, after losing the first set to love. On the third day Budge made things safe for America by beating Quist in three sets. But it was obvious then that without Budge the Americans were going to be hard put to it to beat these Australians again.

Twenty-six nations challenged in 1939, and for the second time some of the matches were played with the shadow of another war moving ominously across the world. In the second round Great Britain beat New Zealand at Brighton by three matches to two, and then triumphed over France at Wimbledon. But in the fourth round against Germany at Berlin, Britain went down by love to five matches. The German team in this match was H. Henkel and R. Menzel in the singles and Henkel and Metaxa in the doubles. The British team was R. A. Hayes and C. E. Hare in the singles and L. Shaffi and F. H. D. Wilde in the doubles. The Germans were then eliminated by Jugoslavia at Zagreb at the end of July by three matches to two, the Yugoslav team consisting of F. Puncec and D. Mitic in the singles and Puncec and Kukuljevic in the doubles.

Australia came through the American zone, and in the inter-zone round beat Yugoslavia by four matches to one. The challenge round between Australia and the holders, the United States, was played at Philadelphia in the first week of September, just as the war was about to start. R. L. Riggs, the new Wimbledon and American champion, was supported by F. A. Parker, ranked Number 5 in the world, in the singles, and by J. A. Kramer and J. Hunt in the doubles. Australia again relied on her two-man team of J. G. Bromwich and A. K. Quist, who were ranked Number 2 and Number 3 in the world respectively. On the first day Riggs beat Bromwich in three sets, and Parker beat Quist in five. With a 2–0 lead America looked set for victory, but the all-conquering doubles pair of Quist and Bromwich made it 1–2, and on the third day Quist levelled the score by a magnificent five-set victory over Riggs, and Bromwich then decided the issue by overwhelming Parker for the loss of only four games. It was really a magnificent performance on the part of the Australians, and very rarely in the history of the Cup has the challenge round been won from a position of love two down on the first day. So once again on the eve of a world war the Davis Cup made the long journey to Australia, as it had done in 1914.

When the competition was resumed in 1946 twenty nations challenged—fifteen in the European zone, four in the American zone, and one, New Zealand, in the Pacific section of the American zone, which was a new introduction into the organisation, though New Zealand did not actually play. Great Britain met France in the first round of the European zone and went down love five, the British team being D. W. Barton and D. MacPhail for the singles and J. S. Oliff and H. Billington for the doubles. Sweden came through as victors of the European zone with a 3–2 win over Yugoslavia in the final round. The inter-zone final between the United States and Sweden was played at New York in September and won by the Americans by five matches to love. Kramer, the Wimbledon and American champion, led his side in the singles with F. A. Parker, the American champion of 1944–45, as second string. The Americans played W. F. Talbert and G. Mulloy, the reigning American champions, in the doubles. Sweden relied on a two-man team of L. Bergelin and T. Johansson.

For their challenge to Australia the United States relied on a two-man team of Kramer and Schroeder in the match which was played at Melbourne at the end of December and resulted in a five love win for the Americans. Australia played Bromwich and D. Pails in the singles and Bromwich and Quist in the doubles. But Australian tennis had not got going again, and the only match which was really close was that in which John Bromwich took Schroeder to five sets on the first day.

Twenty-two nations challenged the United States in 1947. Great Britain beat Poland at Warsaw in the second round of the European zone by three matches to two. Britain's team was A. J. Mottram and D. W. Barton for the singles and G. L. Paish and D. W. Butler for the doubles. Mottram won both his singles and Britain won the doubles in straight sets. In the third round, however, against South Africa, Britain went down by one match to four at Scarborough. E. W. Sturgess, the South African champion, was outstanding, beating both Mottram and Butler in the singles with great ease. Czechoslovakia, led by that fine player, Jaroslav Drobny, were the victors in the European zone, but they were defeated by

Australia in the inter-zone final by four matches to one. John Bromwich, now finding his pre-war form, beat Drobny in straight sets.

The challenge round between Australia and the United States, played at Forest Hills, resulted in a victory for the Americans by four matches to one. Once again America relied on her two-man team of Kramer and Schroeder. The Australian team had Bromwich and Pails again playing the singles and Bromwich and C. F. Long in the doubles. The match was actually closer than the score in matches would suggest. Kramer beat both Pails and Bromwich very easily, but Schroeder took four sets to beat Bromwich, and only managed to beat Pails 6–3, 8–6, 4–6, 9–11, 10–8. Bromwich and Long did splendidly to beat Kramer and Schroeder, the American doubles champions, in the doubles match.

By 1948 the challengers had increased to twenty-five. Great Britain started off the series well by beating India at Harrogate by three matches to two, and then in the second round beating Norway by four matches to one. In the third round, played at Birmingham in the second week of June, Britain beat the Netherlands by four matches to one, which put them into the semi-final—but that was as far as Britain could get. A strong Swedish team beat them at Stockholm in July by four matches to one. For this match Britain relied on her two top players, A. J. Mottram and G. L. Paish, and Sweden also put into the field a two-man team of L. Bergelin and T. Johansson. The only match which Britain won was Mottram's victory over Johansson on the third day. In the final round of the European zone, Sweden went down to Czechoslovakia.

The inter-zone final between Australia and Czechoslovakia was played at Boston in August and was only just won by Australia by three matches to two. As usual the Czechs played their two-man team of J. Drobny and V. Cernik. The Australians were without Bromwich and had a newly constituted team consisting of A. K. Quist and O. W. Sidwell in the singles and C. F. Long and G. E. Brown in the doubles. On the first day Quist beat Cernik, and Sidwell distinguished himself by beating Drobny in four sets. On the second day the Czechs won the doubles and Drobny then beat Quist in a tremendous match—the score being 6–8, 3–6, 18–16, 6–3, 7–5. Sidwell decided the issue by beating Cernik in straight sets, and once again Australia reached the challenge round. Kramer had by now turned professional, and the American singles players were F. A. Parker and F. R. Schroeder with Mulloy and Talbert as the doubles pair. The Australians constituted their doubles team with Sidwell as a partner to Long instead of Geoff Brown. The Americans won with great ease—only the doubles match being a close one.

In 1949 Great Britain played Portugal in the first round of the European zone and won by five matches to love. But in the second round they found Czechoslovakia much too strong. This match was played at Wimbledon and won by the Czechs by four matches to one. Drobny beat both Mottram and Paish in straight sets. The performance of the British pair in the doubles, in which they could only get seven games from Drobny and Cernik, showed British doubles play to be at a very low ebb.

Italy came through the European zone with a final-round victory over France. In the inter-zone final, however, the Italians could not win a match against the growing strength of Australia.

The challenge round at Forest Hills gave the United States a comfortable 4–1 victory. Schroeder beat Sidwell in five sets, and Sedgman in three; and Gonzales, the young American champion, beat Sedgman in a tight three-setter, and Sidwell for the loss of only seven games. The highlight of the tie was Australia's doubles victory on the second day which kept the match alive. On a baking hot day in the Forest Hills stadium, Bromwich and Sidwell beat America's Talbert and Mulloy 3–6, 4–6, 10–8, 9–7, 9–7, in as exciting a doubles match as I have ever seen.

In 1950 seventeen nations challenged, including Pakistan and Israel for the first time. Britain went out to Italy in the first round by two matches to three. The match was notable for a most gallant effort by Britain's second singles player, Geoffrey Paish, in beating R. del Bello in five sets and taking G. Cucelli, who had beaten Mottram in four sets, to 6–8 in the fifth set. But once again it was Britain's doubles weakness which decided the issue.

Sweden won the European zone and contested the inter-zone final with Australia. L. Bergelin, the Swedish stylist, was the hero of this encounter as he beat both Sedgman and Bromwich; but T. Johansson lost both his singles in three sets and the Swedes were no match for Sedgman and Bromwich in the double.

And then, after having lost four consecutive challenges to America, the Australians(49) were at last triumphant and took the Cup back to Australia. Sedgman beat Schroeder and Tom Brown in straight sets, and Ken McGregor did splendidly to beat Schroeder 13–11, 6–3, 6–4 in what was really the key match. Bromwich and Sedgman beat a new pairing of Mulloy and Schroeder in five sets to make the score four matches to one in Australia's favour.

In 1951 twenty-six nations challenged for the Cup. South Africa returned to the competition after a year's absence, and Germany and Japan were allowed to compete for the first time since the war. This was three years quicker than after World War I, after which Germany was not allowed to compete for nine years. Under amended regulations the eight nations which reached the quarter-finals of the European zone the year before were exempted from the first round, and overseas nations wishing to compete in Europe were limited to four.

Britain met France in the second round at Wimbledon and won by three matches to two, but they went right out to Sweden at Scarborough in the next round by love to five. Sweden had twice since the war reached the inter-zone round and were to do so again this year. Their star performer, L. Bergelin, took all five sets to beat Mottram, but overcame Paish in three. The second Swedish singles player, however, Sven Davidson, one of the most improved players in Europe, beat both Mottram and Paish in four sets. Bergelin and Davidson won the doubles 2–6, 6–3, 9–7, 10–8.

In the inter-zone round the United States, thirsting for their revenge over Australia, swept Sweden aside 5–0, and only went down to the holders at Melbourne by the odd match. Australia, against the strong advice of their astute non-playing captain, Harry Hopman, played the young left-hander, Mervyn Rose, in place of Ken McGregor for the second single, and Rose, overawed by the occasion, lost both his singles to Schroeder and Seixas. But Frank Sedgman, the new American champion and the acknowledged Number 1 in the world, was magnificent, winning both his singles matches in the grand manner and pairing with McGregor for yet another great doubles victory over Schroeder and Tony Trabert(47).

And so to 1952. In the second round Britain met Yugoslavia, the British team being Dr. Colin Gregory (captain), the usual two stalwarts, Mottram and Paish, and young Roger Becker, who was being given his first experience of international tennis. Geoffrey Paish, playing second single for Britain, had an accident during his single on the first day and was unable to play in the double. Gregory had to make a big decision as to whether he should put in young Becker to play what might be the deciding match, or whether he should play himself. Despite the fact that he was then forty-six years of age and had only played about two serious games during the past year, he wisely decided to play himself, and gave Mottram magnificent support to win the doubles match, and see Britain through into the third round.

Britain was beaten in this round by Italy at Bologna by four matches to one. Mottram opened against R. del Bello on a baking hot day and failed to win a set. Paish followed against Gardini, a strong hard court player who had beaten Mottram for the loss of only ten games in the French Championships. He beat Paish easily 6–2, 6–3, 6–3. Mottram and Paish put up one of their best ever doubles performances in beating their old enemies, G. Cucelli and M. del Bello 6–3, 6–1, 6–8, 6–2, to keep the match alive.

On the third day, when Mottram won the first two sets against Gardini, it looked as though Britain would draw level. But Mottram was tiring fast and was also attacked by cramp. In the last three sets he could put up little resistance. Anyway Britain had the satisfaction of going out to what was certainly the strongest European nation of the year. Mottram and Paish had served Britain well in her particularly lean and difficult period since the war. For several years they had had to bear the whole burden of singles and doubles. Mottram had played twenty-four Davis Cup singles for Britain, winning sixteen of them, and Paish had put up some very gallant performances.

Italy beat Belgium in the final of the European zone, and then beat India, the Eastern zone finalists. In the inter-zone final, played in Sydney, Australia, in December, the United States beat Italy and thus once again earned the right to challenge Australia for the Cup. Enormous interest was displayed all over the world in this seventh challenge round since the war between these two leading lawn tennis playing nations.

Australia were, of course, favourites to retain the Cup, and they were now well on top of the lawn tennis world and looked likely to remain there. First of all they had the world's leading player in Frank Sedgman—still only twenty-four years of age. To support him as second player they had a choice of two players, both capable of beating anyone. First, tall, gangling Ken McGregor, the holder of the Australian championships; and, second, the brilliant left-hander, Mervyn Rose, aged twenty-two. Rose had beaten R. Savitt, the title-holder, in the Wimbledon Championships and had, in 1951, been preferred to McGregor to play the second singles for Australia in the challenge round. But Harry Hopman, the Australian non-playing captain, was determined that this should not happen again, and, as he had been proved right by the outcome of events the year before, it was quite certain that this time McGregor would play second single.

But behind their top three players Australia had a couple of brilliant youngsters in seventeen-year-old Ken Rosewall and eighteen-year-old Lewis Hoad, who individually and in partnership had done great things during their first year in international tennis. In the American National Champion-ships Rosewall had beaten Seixas, the American Number 1, and Hoad had beaten Art Larsen, the American champion of 1950.

The Australian team was eventually announced as Sedgman, McGregor, Mervyn Rose and Lewis Hoad, although it was almost certain, barring accidents, that Sedgman and McGregor would play the whole match between them. Similarly the Americans were almost certain to play Seixas and Tony Trabert, both in singles and doubles, although they had in reserve Hamilton Richardson and Straight Clark as additional members of their team.

Although Sedgman was the acknowledged Number 1 player in the world, and the Sedgman-McGregor partnership one of the greatest doubles teams of all time, there were certain lines along which American supporters built up their hopes. In the Pacific South-West tournament, played at Los Angeles shortly after the American Championships, Vic Seixas of Philadelphia beat Sedgman in three straight sets—the first defeat the latter had suffered in a major tournament on grass since early 1951. Then in the Queensland Championships, played at Sydney in early November, Sedgman had had to battle all the way to beat Ken Rosewall. In the interzone final of the Davis Cup, played at Sydney in December, Vic Seixas and Tony Trabert showed remarkably good combination when playing together for the first time. They defeated the strong Italian team of G. Cucelli and M. del Bello with the greatest of ease. Tony Trabert, still only twenty-two years of age and in process of doing his military training with the United States Navy, though short of training and match play, was celebrated for his fine physique and tough fighting spirit, and in the American Nationals of 1951 had been the only player to take Sedgman to five sets.

There was another circumstance which might well have affected the play of the two top Australian players. I had been informed on good authority as early as September that all the arrangements had been agreed upon for Sedgman and McGregor to turn professional and join Jack Kramer's "circus" as soon as the Davis Cup challenge round had been played. Despite the fact that everything possible had been done to keep this matter dark, news of it had got out well before the challenge round was played, and there were a certain number of "purists" in the lawn tennis world who thought that Sedgman and McGregor should not have been allowed to play in this match as it was their known intention to turn professional as soon as it was over. This was really complete nonsense as in many former cases—such as Perry of Britain and Donald Budge of America—the same sort of situation had occurred, and it was common property that they were going to turn professional after assisting their country in the challenge round. However, in contests such as this, where nerves play such an important part, matters which are bound to be rather worrying for the principals might possibly have affected their play.

At any rate, what with one thing and another, America's supporters managed to find some grounds for optimism, and Victor Seixas, the American captain, appeared if anything to be rather over-confident—but perhaps he was only whistling to keep up his courage. I think what most people forgot was that players like Sedgman and McGregor, who play a very vigorous all-court net attack game, cannot possibly—and wisely do not try to—put out their very best except on the major occasion.

On the first day the two number ones, Frank Sedgman and Victor Seixas, met one another in the opening match, and from the very start it was apparent that Sedgman was in his finest form, and there was never a moment when the issue was in doubt. Sedgman did not let up for a moment and was the complete master of the forecourt in winning 6–3, 6–4, 6–3.

But the real surprise was the fine form shown by McGregor in the second single against Tony Trabert. McGregor is always a great server, smasher and volleyer, but his very clumsy-looking ground strokes sometimes let him down badly; when these were bad they were really horrid, but, on the other hand, when they were coming off they were so unexpected in their length and their direction that they could hardly have been more difficult for the advancing volleyer.

In this match McGregor played probably better than he had ever done before through the whole of his career, and it was rather ironic that he should have signed on in the professional ranks without winning either Wimbledon or Forest Hills—and at a considerably lower starting price than Sedgman—when, had he played a few more matches like this, he might well have reached the top of the amateur world and been a more expensive proposition for his promoters. Be that as it may, even such a tough player as Trabert soon became utterly exhausted in the great heat in which this match was played, and in trying to compete with someone who was playing all the time just too well for him. After losing a terrific first set at 9–11, Trabert gradually faded right out and eventually had to be almost carried off the court.

The outlook for American supporters as the second day's play started was gloomy in the extreme, to say the least of it—and with every justification. The great team of Sedgman and McGregor, which for more than two years had been right on top of the world, went into action immediately with crushing effect. Seixas and Trabert struggled nobly, and, during a brief period of loss of concentration on Sedgman's part, managed to take the third set. But it was very soon all over, and the Australian victory could hardly have been more complete or more overwhelming.

I never attach much importance to the matches in either the Davis Cup or the Wightman Cup which are played when the result has been decided and the nervous stress removed, and it would indeed have been difficult in such circumstances, with the immediate prospect of their professional tour ahead of them, for Sedgman and McGregor to have given their all in the remaining two matches. As it turned out Sedgman beat Trabert in three sets, and McGregor lost to Seixas.

I cannot conclude this chapter on the Davis Cup without paying a tribute to the Australian non-playing captain, Harry Hopman, for the very great part he had played in these Australian victories—and indeed in the training and coaching of Australia's champions and coming players. Harry Hopman was certainly a hard taskmaster—he asked for the best, and he insisted on getting it. He demanded a standard of physical fitness and stroke perfection in his team higher than that of any other Davis Cup captain I have ever met. He was a most excellent judge of fitness and of form. In the training period he was an inspiration, a guide, philosopher and friend to his team; and when the all-important match took place he was cool and astute, never rattled, fair and sportsmanlike but never giving anything away—and, in my opinion, the greatest non-playing Davis Cup captain in the history of the game.

No leading lawn tennis nation has ever before had to suffer the sudden loss of her two top players when both of them were under the age of twenty-five. Only Australia could suffer such a loss and yet have such splendid reserves of youth at her disposal that she could look upon the future defence of the Cup with good prospects of success.

Chapter Six

THE WIGHTMAN CUP

THE WIGHTMAN CUP—unlike the Davis Cup for men, which is an international event—is a private battle between the women of Britain and the women of America. The Cup was given by Mrs. Hazel Hotchkiss Wightman(50) of Boston who, in the year immediately preceding the First World War, was one of America's great women players, winning the American singles championship four times and the doubles six times. The competition is played alternately in Britain and America each year and consists of seven matches—five singles and two doubles—played off on two consecutive days. Each team nominates three singles players and two doubles pairs; so the teams must consist of a minimum of four players. On the first day the two top singles players on either side play one another and there is a doubles match. On the second day the two top singles players play one more singles each, the third singles players play one another and the second doubles match is played.

Each team has a captain—generally a non-playing captain —who, whilst the matches are in progress, sits by the umpire's chair to advise and encourage the players. From 1923, when the matches first started, up to 1931, Mrs. Wightman was a playing member of the American team. Then for eighteen years she officiated as non-playing captain, and throughout that long period she was the inspiration of women's tennis in the United States.

The first Wightman Cup match was played in 1923 at the inauguration of the new tennis stadium of the West Side Lawn Tennis Club at Forest Hills(54), and it resulted in a win for America by seven matches to love. At that time Mlle

50   Two famous players and rival Wightman Cup captains, at Wimbledon in 1948. Mrs. Kay Menzies (G.B.)
and Mrs. Hazel Hotchkiss Wightman (U.S.A.)

52 Mrs. Jean Walker-Smith, Britain's leading player in 1952 and ranked in the world's top ten

51 Mrs. Jean Bostock, a British player of real class since the war

Suzanne Lenglen, at the height of her form, was the Wimbledon champion—the runner-up that year being Miss Kitty
McKane of Great Britain, who was leading the British side
in this Wightman Cup match. But a young American girl,
Miss Helen Wills, who was to win the American championship that year for the first time, beat Miss McKane and
Mrs. Clayton in straight sets—as did the reigning American
champion, Mrs. M. Mallory. In the doubles Mrs. Wightman
and Miss Goss (America) beat Miss McKane and Mrs.
B. C. Covell 10–8, 5–7, 6–4—a grand match—and Mrs.
Mallory and Miss Wills beat Mrs. Beamish and Mrs. Clayton
6–3, 6–2.

This rather unexpected and total reverse put the British
team on their metal and, in the next year's match, played at
Wimbledon on June 18th and 19th, Britain won by six matches
to one. The British team was considerably remodelled. Mrs.
Covell came in as the second singles player; Miss McKane
was partnered by Miss Evelyn Colyer in the first double, and
Mrs. Covell and Mrs. Shepherd-Barron played the second
double.

Miss McKane, at the very peak of her form, beat the ex-
American champion, Mrs. Mallory 6–3, 6–3, and the reigning
American champion, Miss Helen Wills 6–2, 6–2, a really
great performance. Mrs. Covell also beat them both—
possibly an even greater performance from one of the most
modest, as well as one of the best, British players of her time.
In the doubles Miss McKane was taking under her wing one
of the Wimbledon "babes" who, the year before, had even
shaken for a few games the august partnership of Mlle
Lenglen and Miss Ryan. They took a set from Mrs. Wightman and Miss Wills, the Wimbledon and American title
holders—and hunted them all the way home. In the second
double Mrs. Covell and Mrs. Shepherd-Barron (Great
Britain) beat Mrs. Jessop and Miss Goss 6–2, 6–2. This
British doubles pair might have been one of the strongest
British combinations of the inter-war years with the possible
exception of Mrs. Watson and Mrs. Michell. But they failed
to stick together—the first essential for a really effective
doubles pair.

Britain consolidated her victory in 1925, when the gallant

veteran, Mrs. Lambert Chambers, returned to the fray to win the third single for Britain and to partner Miss Harvey in a winning doubles pair. Twenty-two years before, Mrs. Lambert Chambers had won the Wimbledon singles title for the first time. And Miss McKane steered her young partner, Evelyn Colyer, to a brilliant victory over Miss Wills and Miss Browne 6–0, 6–3.

In 1926 America turned the tables at Wimbledon. Their team was led by Miss Elizabeth Ryan who was probably the best woman player who never succeeded in winning the Wimbledon singles title, but she did win more doubles championships at Wimbledon than anyone before or since. She beat Miss Fry (Great Britain) very comfortably, but lost to the gallant Mrs. Godfree, who also beat Miss Browne—as did Miss Fry. In the third singles, however, Mrs. Jessop (U.S.A.) just beat Mrs. Shepherd-Barron in three sets, and with America winning both doubles, the contest went against us.

In 1927 America won at Forest Hills by five matches to two. The matches Britain won were the third single, in which Miss Betty Nuthall beat Miss Helen Jacobs, and the second double, won by Mrs. John Hill and Miss Gwen Sterry.

In 1928 Britain squared the total account at three all when she won at Wimbledon 4–3. A new and very glamorous star had arisen for Britain in Miss Eileen Bennett. Like Miss Gussie Moran twenty years later, Miss Bennett was apt to be under-rated as a tennis player because of the glamour of her appearance, but she was actually a very fine player indeed and achieved a place as high as Number 3 in a world ranking.

The 1929 match, played at Forest Hills on August 8th and 9th, was just as close as its predecessor, but this time the odd match went to America, who then led by four ties to three. Miss Betty Nuthall, who the following year was to become the only Englishwoman ever to win the American championship, ran Miss Helen Wills to two 8–6 sets; and Mrs. Watson, now ranked as the second player in the world, beat Miss Helen Jacobs, whose world ranking was then Number 3, by 6–3, 6–2. Both the British doubles pairs were victorious. Mrs. Watson and Mrs. Michell easily beat Miss Wills and

Miss Cross (U.S.A.), and Mrs. Covell and Mrs. Shepherd-Barron, playing better than ever, beat Mrs. Wightman and Miss Jacobs for the loss of only three games. These were great days for Britain's women's doubles.

But back came Britain in 1930 to win by the odd match at Wimbledon in as exciting a match as the year before. Mrs. Watson again beat Helen Jacobs, but this time with much more difficulty. Needless to say, Mrs. Helen Wills-Moody won both her singles. Again Britain's doubles came to the rescue. Miss Harvey and Miss Fry beat Miss Cross and Miss Palfrey, and Mrs. Godfree and Mrs. Watson beat Mrs. Wills-Moody and Miss Jacobs—both these matches going the full distance.

Britain had now won the Cup four times and there was nothing in it either way, despite the fact that the great Helen Wills-Moody could almost always be counted upon for two wins on her own. But America now started to draw away, winning the 1931 contest at Forest Hills by five matches to two. Once again our two wins were the doubles matches in which Mrs. Whittingstall (Eileen Bennett) and Miss Nuthall —who had won the American doubles for Britain that year— beat Mrs. Wills-Moody and Mrs. Harper; and Mrs. Shepherd-Barron, now partnered by Miss Mudford, with whom she had won the Wimbledon doubles that year, beat Mrs. Wightman and Miss Palfrey.

On their home courts at Wimbledon in 1932 Britain once more delivered the strongest counter-attack and only went down eventually by three matches to four. In this year Miss Dorothy Round appeared for the first time in the British team. Our three matches were won by Mrs. Whittingstall, who scored a fine victory over Miss Helen Jacobs, and by Mrs. King (Miss Mudford) who beat Mrs. Harper; and we also scored a splendid doubles victory when Miss Nuthall and Mrs. Whittingstall beat Mrs. Wills-Moody and Miss Sarah Palfrey at 10–8 in the final set of the first double.

The 1933 match at Forest Hills proved another victory for America. This year Britain's two top singles players were Miss Dorothy Round, who had reached the final at Wimbledon and taken a set off the great Helen Wills-Moody, and the left-hander, Miss Peggy Scriven, who had won the French singles championship that year. Miss Helen Jacobs, however, was too good for Miss Round, but only just managed to beat Miss Scriven. Miss Sarah Palfrey, America's second singles player, beat Miss Scriven very comfortably but lost to Miss Round. Britain scored another victory when Miss Betty Nuthall beat Miss Babcock in the third single. Miss Nuthall and Miss Freda James scored one more point for Britain when they won the second double against Miss Alice Marble and Mrs. van Ryn.

In 1934, on the Wimbledon courts, America won by five matches to two, and were now leading by eight ties to four. And from this time on it was one long succession of American victories. It was in this year that Miss Dorothy Round beat Miss Helen Jacobs to win the Wimbledon singles title, but in the Wightman Cup match, which was played on June 15th and 16th, before the championships started, Miss Helen Jacobs had beaten Miss Round in two straight sets; and she also easily beat Miss Peggy Scriven, who, for the second year running, had won the championship of France. Miss Sarah Palfrey (U.S.A.), now ranked Number 4 in the world, played second string for America to beat Miss Round and Miss Scriven in two tremendous three-set matches. Once again, however, the gallant Betty Nuthall notched a point for Britain by beating Miss Babcock in the third single. In the doubles Britain's top pair, Mrs. Godfree and Miss Nuthall, just lost to Miss Jacobs and Miss Palfrey; but a new doubles pair, Miss Nancy Lyle and Miss Evelyn Dearman, won the second double for Britain.

Nineteen thirty-five saw Mrs. Helen Wills-Moody back in the fray again as the Wimbledon champion and top of the world of women's tennis, but she did not take part in the American Championships or the Wightman Cup. Her place in the latter was taken by Miss Helen Jacobs, who had been runner-up to her at that year's Wimbledon and had so nearly beaten her in the final. For Britain a new star had arrived in the person of the attractive, hard-hitting left-hander, Miss Kay Stammers, and she immediately made her mark in the Wightman Cup by beating Miss Helen Jacobs in the top single when the two countries met again that year at Forest Hills on August 16th and 17th. Miss Jacobs, however, beat Miss

Dorothy Round with great ease. The second American single player, Mrs. Arnold, lost to Miss Round but beat Miss Stammers. Mrs. Palfrey-Fabyan, whose singles play had improved every year, beat Mrs. M. R. King for the loss of only three games. So America were one up on the singles. In the first double Miss Jacobs and Mrs. Fabyan were too strong for the Wimbledon title-holders, Miss Stammers and Miss James; but Britain's good second doubles pair, Miss Lyle and Miss Dearman, won their match in three sets.

The 1936 match, played at Wimbledon, was almost a repetition of 1935; and once again America just won by the odd match. Miss Jacobs, then ranked Number 1 in the world, was beaten both by Miss Stammers and by Miss Round. Mrs. Fabyan also lost to Miss Round, but beat Miss Stammers; and the vital third single went to America when Miss Babcock beat Miss Mary Hardwick in three sets. American doubles play had been getting stronger and stronger and in this match they won both the doubles—Miss Jacobs and Mrs. Fabyan again beating Miss Stammers and Miss James, while this time Miss Dearman and Miss Lyle fell in three sets to Mrs. J. van Ryn and Miss Babcock.

With the advent of Miss Alice Marble to the ranks of the American singles players the scales started to be weighted more heavily in favour of America and, in the 1937 match, played at Forest Hills, America won by six matches to one. Miss Marble beat Miss Hardwick and Miss Stammers—as also did Miss Helen Jacobs. Mrs. Fabyan easily beat Miss Margot Lumb in the third singles, and the only match won by Britain was the second double in which Miss Stammers and Miss James beat Mrs. van Ryn and Miss Bundy.

The 1938 match, played at Wimbledon on June 10th and 11th, was another repetition, with Mrs. Helen Wills-Moody returned to the American team in place of Miss Helen Jacobs. Miss Kay Stammers covered herself with glory by beating Miss Alice Marble in the top match, but Miss Scriven, who was playing second single in place of Miss Hardwick, lost both to Miss Marble and Mrs. Wills-Moody; and although Miss Stammers battled nobly against the latter she failed to do more than take a set. This year, however, Miss Lumb, a much improved player, took a set off Mrs. Fabyan in the third single and Britain notched another point when Miss Dearman and Miss Ingram succeeded in beating Mrs. Wills-Moody and Miss Bundy in two sets.

In 1939, the last match before the war was played at Forest Hills on August 25th and 26th; and again America won by five matches to two. Miss Helen Jacobs returned to the American side in place of Mrs. Wills-Moody, and Miss Hardwick was back in the British side instead of Miss Scriven. For the third single Britain played a new and promising young player in Miss V. E. Scott. Britain's only two points were won in singles where Miss Stammers again beat Miss Helen Jacobs and Miss Scott put up a splendid first performance in beating Mrs. Fabyan in two straight sets.

So when World War II began America had won the Cup thirteen times to Britain's four and had won the last nine contests off the reel.

When the Cup matches were restarted in 1946 British tennis had been crippled by the war whilst women's tennis in America had continued intensively throughout. It was only to be expected, therefore, that for some years at least it would be all America.

In the first tie, which was played at Wimbledon as usual before the championships, Britain relied for her two top singles on Mrs. Bostock, who, as Jean Nicoll had been the very promising junior champion just before the war(51), and Mrs. Kay Menzies, who had been ranked Number 2 in the world in 1939. They were opposed by Miss Pauline Betz, American champion from 1942 to 1944, and the American and Wimbledon champion-to-be of 1946, and that fine player, Miss Margaret Osborne. The Americans won all the top singles without the loss of a set. The best performance for Britain was put up by Miss Joan Curry in the third single when she ran Miss Louise Brough to 8–6, 6–3. Both the doubles matches were practically a walk-over for America. Miss Brough and Miss Osborne, who had already won the American title four years running, and were to continue to do so until 1951, were much too good for Mrs. Bostock and Mrs. Halford; and Britain's second doubles pair, Mrs. Passingham and Miss Molly Lincoln, could only get four games from Miss Betz and Miss Hart.

In the 1947 match at Forest Hills Britain certainly put up a much better performance but still failed to win a match. Mrs. Bostock took a set from Miss Osborne, as did Mrs. Hilton from Miss Hart. But Britain's post-war doubles play was lamentably weak. Her two youngsters, Miss Gannon and Miss Quertier, could only take three games from Mrs. Todd and Miss Hart; and Mrs. Bostock and Mrs. Hilton could make no real impression on Miss Brough and Miss Osborne.

In the 1948 match at Wimbledon the British women showed still further improvement and Mrs. Bostock and Mrs. Blair scored a glorious victory over Mrs. Todd and Miss Hart, the Wimbledon doubles holders, by 6–3, 6–4. But then came the departure from championship tennis owing to family reasons of Mrs. Jean Bostock, who was the only player of real class Britain had had since the war—with the exception, of course, of Mrs. Menzies who, before the war, was a match for anyone in the world.

The result of the 1949 match, which was played at Philadelphia on August 10th and 11th, was another seven to love victory for America. So overwhelming was the American superiority that, in the first four matches which decided the fate of the Cup, not only did Britain fail to win a set, but they did not get more than three games in any one of the sets played. Our top doubles pair of Mrs. Blair and Miss Quertier were completely overwhelmed and outclassed by Miss Hart and Miss Fry, who were really not such a strong pair at that time as Miss Hart and Mrs. Todd, whom Mrs. Blair and Mrs. Bostock had beaten in the Wightman Cup only the previous year.

The procession of defeats continued in 1950, when once again America won by seven matches to love. From the British point of view the only bright spot was the courageous resistance put up to Miss Brough—who was the Wimbledon champion for the third year running—by Mrs. Betty Hilton, who fought her all the way to five-all in the final set.

At Boston in August of the following year America retained the Cup by six matches to one, this being their fifteenth successive victory in the series. Britain's last success had been in 1930. Our two top singles players were Miss Jean Quertier and Mrs. Walker-Smith (52). The former put up a very creditable performance on the first day against Miss Hart, the Wimbledon title-holder, and Mrs. Walker-Smith struggled nobly against Miss Fry. Mrs. Mottram and Miss Ward, after a good start, were beaten by a rather moderate American pair in Mrs. Todd and Miss Nancy Chaffee. With America leading three matches to love, the sixteen-year-old little Maureen Connolly came on court to play the third single against Britain's Kay Tuckey, who in practice had been playing at the top of her form. To those who had not seen her before Miss Connolly's play was an absolute revelation and there was never a moment in the match when she caused her supporters any anxiety. So once more, by winning the first four matches, America had made certain of the Cup. Then, however, came a welcome break for Britain. Mrs. Walker-Smith put up a magnificent performance by taking a set from Miss Hart and hunting her home all the way; and Miss Jean Quertier gave Britain her first singles victory since the war by beating Miss Shirley Fry in two straight sets.

In 1952 the twenty-fourth Wightman Cup match was played at Wimbledon on June 13th and 14th, resulting in an overwhelming victory for the United States, thus giving them a total of twenty wins in the series against four of ours. For this contest the U.S.A. nominated their team early. It consisted of Miss Maureen Connolly, the fabulous "Little Mo" who had won the American championships the previous year at the age of sixteen; Miss Doris Hart, the 1951 Wimbledon champion; Miss Shirley Fry, the runner-up the year before at Wimbledon and at Forest Hills; and Mrs. Nancy Chaffee-Kiner. The latter withdrew later from the team and her place was taken by Miss Louise Brough, Wimbledon singles champion of 1948–50 and one of the greatest players in the history of the game. The British team consisted of Mrs. Jean Walker-Smith, Mrs. Jean Rinkel-Quertier, Miss Susan Partridge, Mrs. Joy Mottram, Miss Pat Ward and Miss Helen Fletcher. All of these players, with the exception of Miss Partridge, had been members of the team which had lost 1–6 to the United States at Boston the year before.

The American team, though on paper greatly superior to the British was, in my opinion—and as I stated in print before the match—the weakest put out by the U.S.A. since the war.

The great Brough-du Pont combination was missing, and Miss Brough had obviously not recaptured her 1950 championship form. She had, in fact, just previously been beaten by Mrs. Rinkel-Quertier. Miss Hart and Miss Fry were clearly stale from too much tennis—the penalty imposed by the ubiquitous aeroplane. They had just been beaten at Manchester by Miss Brough and Miss Connolly, who had gone down the week before at Surbiton to Mrs. Rinkel-Quertier and Miss Helen Fletcher. Miss Connolly, though a great little player in the making, had sustained recent defeats at the hands of Miss Brough and Mrs. Todd. So the American team was distinctly vulnerable. But the Wightman Cup is always a match in which nerves play a very important part—and at all the critical moments of the match American nerve remained steady and British nerve wilted.

On the all-important first day much depended on Britain's most brilliant player, Mrs. Rinkel-Quertier, who was engaged in two of the three matches. Mrs. Rinkel-Quertier, both in singles and doubles, had been showing world-beating form. Alas, on the all-important day she proved but a pale shadow of her true self and could only take six games from an almost equally nervy Miss Hart. It was a very poor opening match lasting only thirty-five minutes, and even the crowd of schoolgirls could scarcely raise a cheer. In her doubles match Mrs. Rinkel-Quertier was almost equally ineffective, and, despite some virile play by Miss Helen Fletcher, the British pair went down in straight sets to Miss Hart and Miss Fry. Nevertheless, in Mrs. Rinkel-Quertier and Miss Fletcher Britain had a real doubles pair in the making.

It was left to the very gallant Mrs. Jean Walker-Smith to put up a quite magnificent performance for Britain. Giving every ounce of her heart and nerve and sinew she only went down to the American champion, Miss Maureen Connolly, at 5–7 in the final set. So once again we finished the first day three matches down, and, as had happened every year since the war, we lost the Cup in four straight matches—but not before Mrs. Walker-Smith had played another most courageous match, this time against Miss Hart, now thoroughly roused and keyed to give of her best.

With the Cup already lost Mrs. Rinkel-Quertier showed

some of her true form against Miss Maureen Connolly; and then followed the last two matches over which it is best, for Britain, to draw a veil. Miss Susan Partridge, playing third single for Britain against a stale and lethargic Miss Fry, was unbelievably bad and lulled Miss Fry into a coma; though Miss Partridge proved later, in the championships, that this was not really her true form when she gave Miss Connolly the fright of her life in the fourth round of the singles, and might well have defeated her.

In the doubles Mrs. Rinkel-Quertier and Miss Fletcher showed they had the makings of a real pair when they ran Miss Fry and Miss Hart to 6–8, 4–6 in the first double, but in the second double Mrs. Mottram and Miss Ward put up no show at all against Miss Brough and Miss Connolly.

A great many explanations have been given for the poor showing made by British Wightman Cup teams since the war. For the first few years the explanation was a perfectly simple one; there had been a complete gap in British tennis during the war years, and in America the leading women had played and practised intensively. The heavy defeats suffered by Britain's women players in the first years after the competition restarted seemed to give them a moral inferiority, with the result that they were, in many cases, almost beaten before they went on to the court. Mrs. Bostock and Mrs. Blair in doubles, and Mrs. Bostock and Mrs. Hilton in singles, showed what could be done, and by 1952 the gap between the two nations in women's tennis was more apparent than real. But there was no excuse for the poor showing put up by every British doubles pair after the war, with the exception of Mrs. Bostock and Mrs. Blair. The top Americans played intensively, both in practice and in match play, with the same partner, whereas our players were constantly changing from one partner to another. At every crisis, therefore—and one occurs in a first-class double in almost every set—it was just that lack of confidence in themselves and in one another which proved a vital handicap to the British girls.

Chapter Seven

THE GREATEST PLAYERS
OF ALL TIME

WHEREVER FOLLOWERS OF ANY particular sport
meet together on social occasions, or when championships are taking place, the conversation always
turns to comparisons between contemporary champions and
between past and present champions. And despite the fact
that many of the theories advanced can never be put to the
proof and must always be matters of opinion the arguments
continue with unabated vigour. Was Bradman a greater
batsman than W. G. Grace or Jack Hobbs? Who really was
the fastest bowler who has ever played? What would Jack
Johnson in his prime have made of the 1952 heavyweight
champion of the world, Rocky Marciano? Were Davies and
Kershaw the greatest pair of half-backs who have ever played
for England at Rugby football and was there a greater
forward ever in the four countries than "Wakers" Wakefield?
Could the great Doherty brothers, supreme in the world of
lawn tennis in their day, have held their own with the dynamic
forecourt attack of Frank Sedgman? These, and many other
similar controversies, will continue so long as sport is played.
Where exact contemporaries are concerned the matter can,
of course, be proved to a certain extent by the results of
actual matches. But even there no exact deductions may be
possible.

To take one example from the 1951 and 1952 lawn tennis
seasons; on a slow hard court Jaroslav Drobny was the
supreme master; the lack of pace of the ball off the ground
seemed to give him just that extra fraction of a second to
keep the strings of his racket in contact with the ball, by

means of which he could impart to it exact control of place-
ment and spin. Players like Norman Brookes and John
Bromwich sought to achieve the same result on grass by
reducing the tension of their racket strings and so keeping
them in contact with the ball just that fraction of a second
longer. Frank Sedgman, however, almost an exact contemporary of Drobny's, but rather younger in age, was, in
1951 and 1952, just as supreme on a fast grass surface as
Drobny was on the slower hard court. Even in their case it
was difficult to bring them on to one level of comparison.
Still more difficult is it to compare tennis champions of
different eras and of different ages. Yet it is a pastime which
is so popular and so frequently indulged in that no writer on,
or student of, the game can shirk the issue.

Now I will first of all dispose of what is still apt to be a
popular fallacy. Neither in lawn tennis nor in squash rackets
can a woman, however good, compete on level terms in a
single with a man of equal class. I believe that Bill Tilden
did actually play Suzanne Lenglen when both were in their
prime—and the great Suzanne was NOT amused by what
happened. But it did not need that match to prove the truth
of my statement because everyone who has played first-class
tennis or squash knows it for himself. If, however, the
second-class man plays a woman champion at either game
then some very queer things may happen which can reduce
either party to a state of frustration and annoyance beggaring
all description. The woman, by her superiority and accuracy
of stroke, may reduce her male opponent to the state of a
bull rushing madly after an always elusive red rag; or the
man, in his blundering but virile way, may run his skilful
opponent absolutely ragged, until he tramples her exhausted
body underfoot. I have seen both these results from such
mixed encounters—metaphorically speaking, of course. The
doubles game is a different matter. It is really a question of
the court space which has to be covered in a single and it
does explain why the best game of a Miss Betz or a Miss
Connolly, based fundamentally on accuracy and speed of
ground stroke, is likely, over a period, to beat the much more
exhausting game of a Brough or du Pont, relying on the big
service and constant net attack. But against any woman of

slightly lesser class the big game in women's tennis is completely devastating. The same comparisons are not valid in men's tennis because a Borotra or a Sedgman had the physique and strength of leg consistently to cross that dangerous no-man's-land between the baseline and the forecourt and sometimes to hustle the Lacostes and the Sturgesses into defeat by the very vigour and intensity of their net attack.

I have endeavoured to make this chapter easier by classifying at the end of chapters two, three and four, the leading men and women of that particular era of the game's history. But, even so, each era covers the tennis lifetime of two or three generations of players so that procedure can only serve as a rough guide. These classifications must, of course, be largely a matter of opinion—and indeed of controversy and disagreement. But a book on lawn tennis would indeed be dull if it did not provide controversy. A few years ago, in one of the Wimbledon programmes, I published a photo of Mrs. Lambert Chambers in her prime, clad in the high-necked blouse and long skirts of her day. And next door to it I placed a photo of Mrs. Jean Bostock playing at Wimbledon in open-necked vest and the briefest of brief shorts. The caption indicated that Mrs. Lambert Chambers might well have been champion even more times than seven if she had had the advantage of Mrs. Bostock's costume. Mrs. Lambert Chambers, however, didn't agree with me and thought she played better as she was. And maybe she was right.

I would just like to remind my readers of some important points in comparing the champions of different eras. The challenge round at Wimbledon was abolished in 1922. Before that date anyone who was the holder of a championship did not have to compete the next year in the hurly-burly knock-out competition but only had to play the challenge round itself against the winner of the all-comers. This did not involve anything like the physical and mental strain placed upon subsequent champions who had to play all the way through. I very much doubt, for instance, whether a player of such delicate physique as R. F. Doherty could have won the Wimbledon singles four years running if he had been compelled to play through each year.

The game itself has changed very little since the beginning of the twentieth century. The courts perhaps have improved and the balls and the rackets become a little faster and tighter.

Most of the champions, of the last thirty years at least, have become champions by twenty-one, have reached their peak by about twenty-five or twenty-seven, and then have started to decline. There have, of course, been one or two exceptions. Age is therefore a very important matter when making comparisons between champions—particularly since the nineteen thirties.

Merely to estimate the number of championships won by any one player may lead us to false conclusions. It is more important to consider what the opposition was like. For instance, that very unorthodox doubles pair of F. L. Riseley and S. H. Smith twice wrested the Wimbledon doubles from the great Doherty brothers. Two such triumphs might well be worth a dozen championships by other pairs against lesser opponents. Then that great little American hitter, W. M. Johnston, flourished as an almost exact contemporary of an even greater player, W. T. Tilden. What might not Johnston have achieved had it not been for Tilden?

And it must also be remembered that, from 1930 onwards, the champions did not merely, like old soldiers "fade away" —they turned professional. For instance, Kramer should have won Wimbledon at least twice more than he did had he not turned professional after his first triumph in 1947. F. J. Perry, on the other hand, having won Wimbledon three times running—an absolute record since the abolition of the challenge round—had a great player in J. D. Budge treading on his heels and I very much doubt if Perry would have won again. Perry turned pro at exactly the right moment—and thus kept his amateur record intact—if you understand what I mean.

Well then—all these points being taken into account—here are what I consider to have been the greatest players in the world between 1897 and 1952. (I have not gone farther back than 1897 because the competition before then was not great enough to give a fair comparison.)

1. W. T. Tilden	U.S.A.	7. R. A. Gonzales	U.S.A.
2. H. L. Doherty	Great Britain	8. H. Ellsworth Vines	U.S.A.
		9. Henri Cochet	France
3. R. Lacoste	France	10. W. M. Johnston	U.S.A.
4. Norman Brookes	Australia	11. F. J. Perry	Great Britain
5. J. A. Kramer	U.S.A.		
6. Frank Sedgman	Australia	12. Jean Borotra	France

It goes to my heart to leave out such truly great players as J. D. Budge, R. F. Doherty, A. F. Wilding, S. H. Smith, J. C. Parke, M. E. McLoughlin, F. R. Schroeder, A. W. Gore, J. H. Crawford and R. J. Riggs. And I have not included the professionals who did not make the top grade as amateurs. Otherwise F. Segura would have had to be considered. But I shall have something to say about professional lawn tennis in another chapter.

Now I am not going to repeat the performances of all these champions here because I have said a lot about them in previous chapters. I think that most close followers of lawn tennis throughout the years agree that the two super-players in the game's history were W. T. Tilden and H. L. Doherty. They were of two different vintages and of quite different characteristics and it is impossible to compare them directly. Tilden played a great deal more championship lawn tennis than Doherty and for ten years he was unbeaten in a major championship or Davis Cup match. In my opinion, taking all the known factors into consideration, I would place Tilden first and H. L. Doherty second—but there is very little in it and I know opinions differ very much on this point.

René Lacoste was the perfect tennis machine whom many considered to be the best player of all time. He beat Tilden on several occasions but only when that great player was past his best. Lacoste was the most reliable of the famous musketeers of France but the most delicate in health and he gave up the game for this reason when he might have continued for several more years as the world's leading player.

Norman Brookes, the Australian wizard, provided a link between Doherty and Tilden. When he first opposed Doherty in the challenge round of the singles at Wimbledon in 1905 Doherty was nearing the end of his reign as champion and Brookes had not yet reached the peak of his form. Brookes was in the veteran stage when he opposed Tilden in a big match. Yet in 1920 in the challenge round of the Davis Cup, when Brookes was forty-three and Tilden only twenty-seven, Tilden only beat him 10–8, 6–4, 1–6, 6–4; and W. M. Johnston, who massacred G. L. Patterson, the 1919 and 1922 Wimbledon champion 6–3, 6–1, 6–1, could only beat Brookes 5–7, 7–5, 6–3, 6–3. This is what Tilden wrote about Brookes in his book, *The Art of Lawn Tennis*, which was published in 1920 when Brookes's stature as a player was fresh in his memory: "Norman E. Brookes is the greatest match player the world has ever known, because he is ever ready to change his plan to meet the strategy of his opponent, and has both the variety of stroke and versatility of intellect to outguess the other the majority of times. Brookes is the greatest court general and, in my opinion, the finest tennis intellect in the world. His mind is never so keen and he is never so dangerous as when he is trailing in an important match." I have, therefore, some very solid support for placing Norman Brookes at Number 4.

Now I am quite frankly in a dilemma. Where do the modern champions fit into my first dozen—if at all? Any direct comparison is impossible and my other difficulty is that the three I am going to take now all left the amateur competitive ranks when they were still on the up grade; and moreover Jack Kramer's career was interrupted by the war after he had first attained Davis Cup honours. Nevertheless he was such a fine player when he won the Wimbledon and American championships in 1947 that I feel sure he would have won them again at least twice more had he remained in the amateur ranks. I once described Jack Kramer as the Rolls Royce of lawn tennis—smooth, powerful and efficient. His game resembled Tilden's in that it was stroke perfect but it lacked the slice strokes which Tilden cultivated—not that I think Kramer lost anything by that. Kramer volleyed more than Tilden in a single and was a better doubles player. He always kept himself in the very pink of condition and was ever anxious to give of his best. Tilden gave the impression

53 The Centre Court at Wimbledon in 1952. The great Australian doubles pair, McGregor and Sedgman (*right*), playing J. Brichant and P. Washer of Belgium

54   The West Side Tennis Club at Forest Hills, New York, where the American National Championships are played.
In the foreground is the Stadium court.

on court that the crowd were lucky to have the opportunity of seeing him play; Kramer that he was privileged
to be allowed to appear and hoped to give them full value for
their money.

Jack Kramer was modest and unassuming, a great player
and a great sportsman. His type of game was particularly
adapted to the professional circus because he had great control
of the ball and few off days. His record was, of course,
nothing like as great as that of Tilden who for years bestrode
the lawn tennis world like a colossus and had that touch
of genius and sizzling speed which made him completely
outstanding.

Frank Sedgman turned professional at twenty-four when
he was not only the top player in the world but still on the
up and up. In the Davis Cup he had already played eleven
challenge round matches and won nine of them. In the
1950, 1951 and 1952 challenge rounds he won six singles for
the loss of only one set. His form in winning the American
championships of 1951 and 1952 and the Wimbledon of 1952
was really great. Sedgman was, in fact, a modernised version
of Cochet, taking almost as early a ball but adding to Cochet's
game a powerful service and more speed of stroke all round.
Cochet sauntered about the court, juggling with the ball,
nonchalant, utterly confident—often too much so. He seemed
to enjoy letting a match go to five sets and was always most
dangerous when he was behind. Sedgman, a glorious young
athlete, trained like a prize-fighter, came out when the bell
went, to win in three straight sets if he could. Cochet was
the perfect foil to the American "big game", absorbing the
speed of Tilden to his own advantage. Sedgman imposed his
own powerful shock attack on his adversary. Both Cochet
and Sedgman had wonderfully quick reflexes and anticipation. Cochet's were directed by his head; Sedgman's were
instinctive. Cochet was by far the more intelligent of the
two—and in that respect Sedgman is something of an enigma.

Frank Sedgman, like Kramer, was modest, without any
flamboyant mannerisms on court, and a thoroughly straight
and likeable person. He was even better in doubles than in
singles and, considering these two together, may well have
become the greatest all-rounder the game has ever known.

My third modern champion is Gonzales. We only saw him once at Wimbledon and he was certainly not then at his best. But he won the American championships when he was twenty in 1948 and again in 1949. I saw him win at Forest Hills that year and I saw him beat Sedgman in three straight sets in the challenge round of the Davis Cup. He turned professional at only twenty-one when the ball was at his feet in the amateur game.

Gonzales had all the outward essential qualifications of a champion—height, fine physique, blistering speed and a great heart. He had not the tennis brain of a Doherty, a Tilden or a Borotra and was apt to be overcome by his own emotions.

So taking all these factors into consideration I give my fifth, sixth and seventh places in a best-ever world ranking to Kramer, Sedgman and Gonzales.

And now I face a second big dilemma. It is almost inconceivable that Vines, Cochet, Borotra, Perry, Budge, W. M. Johnston, Anthony Wilding, J. H. Crawford and R. L. Riggs should be excluded from such a list—and what about R. F. Doherty? But I have only five more places in my first twelve.

Vines had a short but electric career at the top. He won the Wimbledon singles in 1932 at his first attempt, when he was twenty-one—and in doing so he played the most devastatingly unplayable tennis I have ever seen. In the semi-final he beat J. H. Crawford of Australia, who had beaten F. J. Perry the round before in four sets. Vines beat Crawford for the loss of only six games and swept H. W. Austin off the court in the final. Vines won the American singles in 1931 and 1932 and returned to Wimbledon in 1933. He was not quite in such good form that year, but he beat Cochet for the loss of one set in the semi-final and lost in the final to J. H. Crawford in one of the greatest five-set matches ever seen at Wimbledon. Vines hit an almost completely flat ball with the emphasis on speed. It stood to reason therefore that if his eye and timing were just the slightest bit out he gave away a great number of errors. But when everything was in tune then he played the sort of tennis to which there was no reply. Vines then joined the professional ranks but never took tennis very seriously again and soon transferred his affection to golf, where he became a fine player.

So my eighth place goes to Ellsworth Vines.

My Number 9 is Henri Cochet, who might on his best day have beaten any of the eight names above him, including the great Bill Tilden himself—which he did do on several occasions. From 1928 to 1931 Cochet was ranked Number 1 in the world. But he was not so consistently great as Lacoste, nor had he the crushing power of Sedgman. This is what Tilden said about Cochet in 1928: "His marvellous court covering is not only a remarkable piece of physical control but it is beautiful to watch. He is never awkward, never seemingly hurried unduly in making his strokes. In these inspired moments of his, Cochet is the greatest of all Frenchmen and in my opinion possibly the greatest player who has ever lived." But it must be remembered that when Tilden wrote this he himself had been dethroned and beaten by Cochet. Nevertheless Cochet was a very great player indeed and it may well be that he should have been ranked higher.

For Number 10 I have chosen that great little smiter of a lawn tennis ball, W. M. "Little Bill" Johnston—and it is arguable that he should be Number 5. He was American champion in 1915 and again in 1919, when he beat Bill Tilden in the final. Then Tilden beat him in 1920 and again and again every year from 1922 to 1925—in all of which years Johnston would have been champion of America and of the world had it not been for the super-player who was just on top of him. Johnston's play for America in the challenge rounds of the Davis Cup, after he and Tilden had won it together in 1920, was terrific. His great forehand simply buried the fastest services and drives of such big hitters as Patterson and Anderson of Australia. And even in 1926, eleven years after he had first won the American championship, he was good enough to beat Lacoste 6–0, 6–4, 0–6, 6–0, and Borotra 6–2, 6–3, 6–3, when these two were ranked amongst the foremost players in the world.

My last two places go to F. J. Perry and Jean Borotra. From 1934 to 1936 Perry was the leading world player and the only player since the challenge round was abolished to win Wimbledon three times running. He also won the American championship three times, the Australian championship once and the French championship once. He then turned professional, with Budge, von Cramm and Riggs treading on his heels. There was not much in it between Vines, Perry, Budge and Crawford. At the 1932 Wimbledon Crawford beat Perry, and then Vines easily beat Crawford. At the 1933 Wimbledon Perry fell to N. G. Farquharson in the second round and Crawford just beat Vines in the final. In the 1933 inter-zone round of the Davis Cup Perry beat Vines after the tie was decided. Vines had a fall in the fourth set and retired in the fifth but he had been easily beaten by Austin on the first day, so was obviously not himself—judging him by his 1932 Wimbledon form. Vines had turned professional before the next Wimbledon—which Perry won.

In the 1935 challenge round of the Davis Cup Perry beat Budge in four sets. Budge beat Crawford in the 1936 Davis Cup. And in his last Wimbledon (1936) Perry beat Budge in four sets. Perry usually got the better of Crawford.

After the departure of Perry to the professional ranks Budge was the leading player in the world and in 1938 became the only player in the history of the game to win the championship of Wimbledon, America, France and Australia in the same year.

Perhaps the two most notable omissions from my first twelve are R. F. Doherty and Donald Budge—and they were certainly two of the greatest players ever. Many people thought that R. F. Doherty was a better player than his brother, H. L., but R. F.'s health was not good and I very much doubt whether he would have won Wimbledon four times running as he did do if he had had to play through the event each time. Borotra might well have beaten anyone on my list and did, in fact, beat Lacoste and Cochet, his two great compatriots, on several big occasions; but Borotra could never beat Tilden out of doors as both of the others did. Of all the great players on my list Borotra lasted longest in first-class tennis and enjoyed his tennis most.

MEN'S DOUBLES

1. R. F. and H. L. Doherty
2. W. L. Allison and J. van Ryn
3. A. K. Quist and J. E. Bromwich
4. F. Sedgman and K. McGregor

5. J. H. Doeg and G. M. Lott
6. S. H. Smith and F. L. Riseley
7. J. Borotra and J. Brugnon
8. N. E. Brookes and A. F. Wilding
9. H. Hackett and F. B. Alexander
10. F. Sedgman and J. Bromwich
11. W. T. Tilden and Vincent Richards
12. H. Roper Barrett and C. P. Dixon

Although I believe there are not as many good doubles pairs in modern tennis as there used to be, those which have achieved distinction are very good indeed. It is a toss up whether the much greater intelligence possessed by a pair like the Dohertys could compensate for the power and punch of a couple of highly trained young athletes such as Sedgman and McGregor of Australia, who performed the unique feat of winning all four of the world's major doubles championships in one year.

I have obviously had to leave out some very great pairs such as Crawford and Quist of Australia, Cochet and Brugnon (France), Mulloy and Talbert (U.S.A.), Holcombe Ward and Beals Wright (U.S.A.), Maurice McLoughlin and T. C. Bundy (U.S.A.), and that fine British pair, J. C. Gregory and I. G. Collins. I have not managed to find a place for Jack Kramer whom I rank as one of the finest doubles players of them all. It may be that he and F. R. Schroeder should well deserve a place.

WOMEN'S SINGLES

1. Mlle Lenglen
2. Mrs. Wills-Moody
3. Miss Alice Marble
4. Mrs. Lambert Chambers
5. Miss May Sutton
6. Miss Pauline Betz
7. Miss Louise Brough
8. Mrs. Margaret du Pont
9. Miss Doris Hart
10. Miss Maureen Connolly
11. Mrs. L. A. Godfree
12. Miss Dorothy Round

I think most people would agree that the two outstanding players of all time were Suzanne Lenglen and Helen Wills. They did meet once in 1926 in the final of the Carlton tournament at Cannes, in a match which caused tremendous interest. Suzanne won 6–3, 8–6, but she was then in the last year of her reign and Helen Wills was only on the threshold of her career. So there was really no direct comparison. But those who saw them both at the zenith of their form would, I think, have little hesitation in ranking Mlle Lenglen as the greatest woman player in the history of the game.

Miss Alice Marble is thought by many to have been even greater than Helen Wills, though her style of play was quite different and her achievements were not nearly so great, because the Second World War finished her amateur career before it had even reached its peak. She certainly introduced a style of woman's "big game" which was copied with considerable success by some of her post-war successors but which none of them played quite so well as she did.

Following Alice Marble I have gone back before the First World War to give fourth place to Mrs. Lambert Chambers, seven times Wimbledon champion. It is true, of course, that on some of these occasions Mrs. Lambert Chambers only had to play the challenge round; but she had to play through in 1903, 1906, 1910 and 1913. And don't let's forget her tremendous match with Mlle Lenglen in 1919, five years after she had won her last championship, with the war years between, and *sixteen* years after she had won her first. Mrs. Lambert Chambers surely deserves fourth place. And I have given fifth place to Miss May Sutton of California who came to Wimbledon in 1905, aged only eighteen, and took the title from Mrs. Lambert Chambers at her first attempt. Miss Sutton's career was a short one and she only won one more Wimbledon; but she was without doubt a quite exceptional player. It may be that the fabulous Miss Lottie Dod, who won Wimbledon first in 1887 and, having won four more times, retired from the game altogether, well deserves a place amongst the immortals. She was certainly a most remarkable player but the competition in those days was so small that I have not attempted to go back farther than 1897.

Then come those five great Americans, who dominated the world of women's tennis after the Second World War; Miss Pauline Betz, Miss Louise Brough, Mrs. Margaret du Pont, Miss Doris Hart and Miss Maureen Connolly. Miss Betz, who might well have won Wimbledon several times more had she not turned professional after her first win in 1946, just had the edge on Miss Brough and Mrs. du Pont as they, in turn, had over Miss Doris Hart. Miss Connolly, of course, may shoot several places up the ladder of fame before she has finished. But at the moment her career has only just started. For my eleventh place I take Mrs. Godfree of Great Britain, who, existing, unfortunately for her, in the middle of the Lenglen era, yet won Wimbledon twice. And for Number 12 I have selected another fine British singles player, Miss Dorothy Round, who in an age of many strong women players was champion in 1934 and 1937.

I realise that I have excluded such fine players as Miss Betty Nuthall, Mrs. Menzies, Miss Helen Jacobs, Mrs. Bostock, Mrs. Pat Todd, Mrs. Hillyard, Mrs. Sterry, Fräulein Aussem, Frau Sperling, Miss Martin and Mrs. Larcombe, some of whom have beaten players on my list and might well claim to be included.

WOMEN'S DOUBLES

1. Mlle Lenglen and Miss Ryan
2. Miss Brough and Mrs. du Pont
3. Mrs. Fabyan and Miss Marble
4. Mrs. Todd and Miss Hart
5. Miss Hart and Miss Fry
6. Miss Helen Jacobs and Mrs. Fabyan
7. Miss Ryan and Mme Mathieu
8. Mrs. Watson and Mrs. Michell
9. Miss Nuthall and Mrs. Whittingstall
10. Miss K. Stammers and Miss James
11. Mrs. Wightman and Miss Wills
12. Mrs. Covell and Miss K. McKane (Mrs. Godfree)

Generally speaking I think there has been a deterioration in women's doubles since the Second World War; but three post-war American pairs have been outstanding—Miss Brough and Mrs. du Pont, Miss Hart and Mrs. Todd, and Miss Hart and Miss Fry. It may well be that the third of these pairs may move up a place, but Miss Hart and Mrs. Todd beat the great Brough-du Pont combination for the Wimbledon title when the latter pair were at the height of their glory and strength.

Particularly good pairs I have had to leave out are Mrs.

Shepherd-Barron and Mrs. Covell, Mrs. Shepherd-Barron and Miss Mudford (Mrs. King), Miss Nuthall and Mrs. Fabyan—all of which might have beaten several in my list—Mrs. Bostock and Mrs. Blair, Mrs. Todd and Miss Moran Mrs. Bostock and Mrs. Hilton, and Mrs. Menzies with Mrs. Bostock or Mrs. Blair.

The period 1925–30 was a great one for women's doubles—particularly for Britain—and it may well be that another pair of two from that period should be included in my list.

Chapter Eight

THE PROFESSIONAL
GAME

UNTIL A COMPARATIVELY SHORT time ago there
was only one type of lawn tennis—the amateur game.
This was the game of knock-out competition as
typified by the Wimbledon Championships, and the other
great national championships all over the world. The professionals of lawn tennis were the teachers of the game. In
Britain they are a small and very worthy body, sponsored
and looked after by the British Lawn Tennis Association,
and earning their living by giving lessons either to individuals
or to schools or classes.

Then, in the years between the two world wars, another
class of professional arose—the "play for pay" type. This
kind of professional is recruited from the great players who
have made their names in the amateur ranks. They play for
money prizes in touring groups or "circuses", generally consisting of an economical unit of four men, sometimes with
two women attached to give some glamour and variety to the
proceedings. They generally play indoors by artificial light
so that they are independent of the weather, and so that their
matches can attract, by late evening play, people whose work
does not permit them to watch tennis by daylight. This type
of professionalism affords lucrative prizes for a few years to
a small number of players with big reputations. They can
then revert to the ordinary activities of any other sports
professional—keeping a sports shop, giving lessons, selling
some special form of sports equipment, and so forth. Until
quite recently there was bitter antagonism between the
Amateur Lawn Tennis Associations and the promoters of

the professional circus. Fortunately this is dying down—for in actual fact the two types of game are complementary to one another—as long as each recognises the other's functions and point of view. The professional circus only exists and flourishes, firstly, because of the increasing popularity of amateur lawn tennis as a world game, and secondly, because it has been possible to give the professional game a steady and regular blood transfusion from the ranks of the amateur champions who have made their names in the stern arena of knock-out competition. Without these two essential supports provided by the amateur game the professional "play-for-pay" game would languish. Why is it that throughout 1952 ex-amateur champion, Jack Kramer, was racing and chasing all over the world after the reigning amateur champion, Frank Sedgman, offering him ever bigger inducements to turn professional and join his "circus"? Because the "play-for-pay" public were becoming bored with watching Budge play Kramer, Kramer play Budge, Gonzales play Segura and vice versa, night after night. And, quite frankly, some of these gladiators were getting no younger—and it was heartbreaking for some of his fans to see a forty-year-old Fred Perry trying in vain to emulate his great game of fifteen years before when he could race up to the net like a young stag and conquer the world.

The professional lawn tennis promoters are complete realists with regard to these matters—and they have to be, as do the players themselves, because professional lawn tennis is a hard-headed business proposition.

Now let's take a quite straightforward look at this matter, about which there is such a lot of loose thinking, and see how the professional game in lawn tennis differs, for instance, from golf, with which it is so often compared. Modern lawn tennis in the championship class is one of the most strenuous and exacting sports in the world, demanding youth and the highest degree of mental and physical fitness. J. C. Parke, who was both a lawn tennis and a Rugby football international, was of the opinion that a five-set match at lawn tennis was more exhausting than a Rugby football international. But, be that as it may, there is no doubt about it that tennis is a young man's game. It will be found that in the intense competitive atmosphere of the amateur game a male player reaches his physical peak somewhere about twenty-five or twenty-seven, and a woman slightly earlier. Suzanne Lenglen, Tilden, Helen Wills, Lacoste, Borotra, Vines, Perry, Budge, Riggs, Alice Marble, Louise Brough, Margaret du Pont, Doris Hart, Gonzales and Sedgman were all great players by the time they were twenty-one. And none of them, with the possible exception of Riggs, improved after the age of twenty-five or twenty-seven. It was the intense knock-out competition of the amateur game which spurred them on and kept them at concert pitch. Only Riggs, Segura and Gonzales have actually improved their game in the professional ranks—and they, by force of circumstances, transferred before they had made their best possible reputation in the amateur ranks. Otherwise, the aim of all those amateur champions, who decided to turn professional over the last twenty years, has been to make the transfer when their reputations were at their highest and they could demand the biggest possible transfer fee and the best gates for their matches. Once having turned professional it is the most difficult thing in the world to keep one's game at concert pitch. Advancing years and lack of varied knock-out competition are apt to blunt the edge of any champion's game. Hence the fact that the new professional champions don't come from the professional ranks but from the ranks of the latest amateur champion turned professional. This does not happen in any other game I know. Tilden, Vines, Perry, Budge, Riggs, Kramer and Gonzales each very soon assumed the mantle of leading professional on transfer from the amateur ranks.

Now this is quite different from the game of golf where the ball is stationary and the player does not have to be trained like a prize-fighter to give of his best. Improvement continues with practice and match play, and it is unusual for the leading amateurs to beat the leading professionals, who can remain in the top class into their forties or fifties.

The open tournament, therefore, is a very reasonable and attractive proposition in golf. But where is the demand for it in lawn tennis? Many more people want to go to Wimbledon every year than the place can possibly hold, and the fact that last year's champion has become a professional doesn't make the slightest difference. The up-and-coming young amateurs might like to have a free tilt at the Sedgmans and McGregors, but what would the professional promoters think of the big fish they have taken such trouble to hook being gaffed by some young Rosewall or Hoad? In my experience the people who are least keen on the open tournament are the professionals themselves. And very rightly too. They would have much to risk and little to gain.

Looked at from a commonsense standpoint the present situation with regard to professional and amateur tennis is generally reasonable and satisfactory, and the two games can be, and are, complementary to one another. The bigger the Wimbledon crowds become—and the would-be spectators increase every year—the more demand is there in the big cities and the out-of-the-way places of the earth for a visit from a professional "circus", where, after the day's work is over, people can sit under cover and see lawn tennis played by the world's greatest exponents of the game. The fact that professional "tournaments" held at Wembley are now sponsored by the British L.T.A. shows that a more sensible view is being taken of the whole matter.

After the 1951 challenge round of the Davis Cup big inducements were offered to Frank Sedgman to turn professional and counter-inducements, in the way of jobs and wedding presents, were offered by Australia to get him to remain an amateur. This rather undignified auctioneering was repeated the next year, with the professional promoter always able to offer the big, immediate, glittering prize, which to any young man in his middle twenties is a greater attraction than the security in middle age offered by the amateur body.

Other great amateur champions have had the same sort of decision to make as Sedgman, but most of them had reached the zenith of their amateur careers, and were probably on the way down, when they crossed the Rubicon and joined the professional ranks. Therefore the lawn tennis authorities of their own countries were not so keen on offering financial counter-inducements.

Personally I see this problem as a very simple one of supply and demand, and, as usual in these matters, I find that the customer is generally right. And the customer in this case is the lawn tennis viewing public. They pay their money and they take their choice. Their first attraction without any doubt is the thrill and the colour of knock-out competition such as draws the crowds to Twickenham, to Wembley—and to Wimbledon; the unknown knight who enters the lists and pits his heart, and his nerve, and his sinew and his skill, for one glorious hour, maybe, against the reigning champion. In the cup final at Wembley, in an international rugger match, or at Wimbledon this is the sort of thing for which the public are willing to wait and queue, and pay, and wait again—and cheer. If the customer were not right about Wimbledon the management would be touting for support instead of returning thousands of pounds each year to people who have been unlucky in the ballot for tickets, conducted months before anyone knows what the entry is going to be.

And then there is that other public, which can't get to Wimbledon or Forest Hills but which still wants to see the stars. So many people in so many countries of the world want to see these champions in action that it pays the professional lawn tennis promoters to offer them substantial sums of money to oblige their fans. All power then to the promoters—and good luck to the stars. The whole matter is one of commonsense supply and demand. If the player is not a star with a big name—there is no demand for him from the public. And the skill and courage which can give a lawn tennis player a big name comes, in lawn tennis, from the crucible of knock-out competition which only exists in the amateur game.

Now I know my readers will say: "Is there no element of knock-out competition in the professional game?" Of course there is. A lawn tennis champion has his pride and wishes to give of his best. But when two top class professionals, possibly one newly transferred from the amateur ranks, embark on a world tour in which they are to play one another, say, a hundred times, and both are to get a share of the gate, with the best will in the world, it is difficult to keep up the sort of red-hot keenness which characterises a Wimbledon championship. One or both are apt to get stale—or bored, or even completely physically exhausted. And if one wins every time—what about the gate? And their share of the money? Also, of course, the professional matches are rarely played over the full five-set distance. They are generally the best of three sets—quite a different game—and sometimes only one set is played to get in the whole evening's entertainment.

So we should sympathise with the difficulties of the professional "play-for-pay" coterie. They have a far more difficult problem than the national Lawn Tennis Associations —who merely open the doors and allow the competitors and spectators to crowd in.

Another very interesting question is how the newly transferred ex-amateurs will take to the professional game. The arc-lights, the noisy boards of the playing surface, the linesmen in dinner jackets, even "the dons on the dais serene" actually tucking into a four-course dinner just up above the court, whilst they toil and sweat below, are not every tennis player's cup of tea. And some players don't take to the atmosphere or the playing surface at all. Others require some time to get acclimatised. When Kramer turned professional in 1947 he at first lost to Riggs, the reigning professional champion, but he soon gained a complete ascendancy.

Then the professional "play-for-pay" type must be a good trouper. He must be able to travel from place to place with the portable court surface in the guard's van or the back of the aeroplane and roll it out and give his best turn. Will Frank Sedgman, for example, be able to produce his best under these conditions? I should rather doubt it—but time will give the answer.

The two who, day in and day out, have done best in professional tennis are Bobby Riggs, with his wisecracks and his supreme confidence in himself, and Jack Kramer, the Rolls Royce who always ran smoothly into top gear in almost any circumstances; while Segura and Gonzales, who turned professional before reaching the peak of their game, were anxious to get to the top in their new environment. Curiously enough the amateur player who would, I think, have done almost better than anyone in the professional ranks is Jaroslav Drobny, with his tremendous service and forehand and uncanny control of the ball. But Drobny could never do quite well enough in the big amateur championships to be offered a profitable enough contract. This is really a pity as Drobny would have been a money spinner in the "play-for-pay" ranks.

The expenses allowed to the amateur player have, from time to time, come in for a good deal of criticism—and there has been a lot of talk of "sham-amateurism". Now the tournament lawn tennis player can no more afford to pay his travelling and hotel expenses these days than can a member of a travelling football or cricket side. Otherwise modern lawn tennis would be confined to the leisured classes, as it was years ago. The question which has to be decided by the International Lawn Tennis Federation and the national associations is what expenses are legitimate and what are not. The only real essential differentiation between the professional and the amateur is that one plays for money prizes and a share of the gate and the other does not. In some countries assistance is given to promising young amateur players by arranging for them jobs in sports firms where they can combine their work with playing tennis. The British L.T.A. announced recently that they were going to do more in this line.

There is, I know, a section of opinion which supports the point of view that there should be no differentiation between amateur and professional and that all tournaments should be open. The American and British Lawn Tennis Associations are strongly opposed to this idea, and I cannot see Wimbledon or Forest Hills becoming professionalised. Rugby Union Football and Rugby League Football get along perfectly well together. Every now and then a star performer from the amateur body signs on with the professionals, which benefits the latter and does not affect the former. I think the position in lawn tennis is much the same. If, of course, there was some indication that Wimbledon was losing the support of the public then there might be some argument for making a change. One of the first principles of match play in lawn tennis is "Never change a winning game—always change a losing one." The record crowds at Wimbledon, Forest Hills and Adelaide are evidence of the ever-increasing draw of amateur lawn tennis. The competition grows ever fiercer, and that tends to give more excitement to the spectators and improve the standard of the play. And if those who attain the highest honours in the amateur game choose to cash in on their achievements—what matter? Behind every Sedgman there is a Rosewall, and behind every McGregor a Hoad. And amateur lawn tennis remains, as it always has been, a game of great endeavour, a game of great sportsmanship, and a game which demands both from men and women their highest qualities of skill and endurance.

Chapter Nine

THE WAY AHEAD

PERHAPS THE TWO MOST thorny problems of recent
times on the administrative side of the game have been,
first, the extent to which the interests of governments in
international sport should be recognised, and secondly, the
vexed question of "amateurism", about which I have said
something in the previous chapter. With regard to the interests
of governments, the International Federation has always
regarded it as fundamental that it has no concern with
politics, race or creed. But it is often difficult these days to
keep rigidly to this principle when certain nations and creeds
seek to use the world of sport for the furtherance of their
political aims. Again, there are today a number of first-class
lawn tennis players who, for political reasons, are disowned
by their own governments.

The question of amateurism has, of course, been made
more difficult by the times in which we live—the increased
expense of the game, the vastly increased number of players
and tournaments, and the advent of air travel which takes
the player to the world and brings every world championship
within the reach of any player.

In all these delicate matters the International Lawn Tennis
Federation has very wisely striven to follow public opinion
rather than dictate to it.

Since the beginning of the twentieth century the rules of
lawn tennis and the courts on which it is played have altered
little. But it is in the ever-changing personalities of the
champions that the real history of the game is written: they
have run in all shapes and sizes, and each has brought to the
game something different and something essentially their
own. On the men's side, since the long reign of Tilden ended,

the general development has been along the lines of gaining speed—and time—by the taking of an earlier ball. This type of game was exemplified by Henri Cochet, by Fred Perry and finally by Frank Sedgman of Australia. Sedgman's game is a more powerful edition of Cochet's, and is, I believe, the last word in men's tennis. It is not a very safe game as it gives little margin for error and it may not be very suitable for the professional "circus", where the same players have to oppose one another night after night. Kramer referred to this recently as "the gruelling grind on American boards", and it favours the more controlled game of a Kramer rather than the "flatter" game of a Sedgman. In fact Sedgman's game is essentially one for the big occasion, whereas Kramer's is utility plus. Nevertheless, the young athlete, prepared to give his all in every match, will, I believe, get farther with Sedgman's early-ball-and-up-to-the-net game than with any other. But any other type of player will probably do better to follow Kramer.

On the other hand, the last word in women's tennis was, I believe, produced by Mlle Lenglen, Helen Wills-Moody, Miss Pauline Betz and Miss Maureen Connolly. The "women's big game" produced by the great Alice Marble and carried on by Miss Brough and Mrs. du Pont was, in my opinion, a stormy interlude in women's tennis and not a natural development of the feminine game. Had Miss Betz not departed to the professional ranks after only one victory at Wimbledon, the big game of Miss Brough and Mrs. du Pont might not have had such a long reign. Nevertheless I should personally advise a girl starting on a lawn tennis career to begin by learning first a good service, then the volley and lastly the ground strokes—although the latter must be the bedrock of a woman's game. Most of our British women were taught the other way round—and became wedded to the baseline. On the other hand, the great "Little Mo" Connolly became champion of America almost on her ground strokes alone.

Comparatively few people have realised how much the recent successes of the Australians in the Davis Cup are due to their very exacting régime of physical training. With the exception of boxing, I know of few sports where a high degree of physical fitness pays such dividends as it does in lawn tennis. There have been outstanding examples of this throughout the history of the game. The great New Zealander, Anthony Wilding, trained for Wimbledon and the Davis Cup just as a boxer trains for a prize-fight. The famous Frenchman, Jean Borotra, subjected himself to a most rigorous regular system of physical training throughout the whole of his career, and he puts down much of his success to this fact. Jack Kramer of the United States really trained like a boxer for his big lawn tennis matches. But it was left to Harry Hopman, the architect of recent Australian Davis Cup victories, to take physical training for lawn tennis one step farther. There had always been an idea that physical training in a gym tended to make an athlete muscle bound. I was never quite convinced that it need; and when I travelled over to America with Randolph Turpin on his way to fight Sugar Ray Robinson I became a convinced supporter of scientifically applied muscle development—or perhaps muscle conditioning would be a better word. Turpin has applied these methods to a much greater degree than any boxer I had studied previously, and he did it without in any way reducing his speed of movement or indeed his speed of punch. Harry Hopman, the greatest Davis Cup captain and trainer in the history of lawn tennis, has applied the same sort of methods. He has not only made his team run five miles as a matter of daily routine, but he has built up in them by gymnastic exercise certain muscles which they use for certain strokes. Now in lawn tennis, as in boxing, if one contestant is in a superior class to his opponent, physical condition may not be an important factor. The match, or the contest, will probably be over in too short a time for that factor to count. But when the contestants are evenly matched, then physical condition and toughness are matters of supreme importance. Just recently American Davis Cup teams have been put through a fairly severe course of physical training immediately prior to a cup match, but no other nation has insisted upon such a prolonged period of physical preparation as have recent Australian Cup teams under the direction of Harry Hopman. And this has certainly been one of the secrets of their success.

In the women's ranks, Maureen Connolly has also subjected

herself, under the guidance of her famous coach, Miss "Teach" Tennant, to a physical training régime on and off the court which would have been regarded by her British contemporaries as little short of cruelty to animals. Yet in how many tight matches has her amazing physical fitness pulled "Little Mo" through to victory!

But besides the actual physical training, which is of such great importance in a sport demanding physical excellence of as high a standard as any other in the world, there is the equally important matter of stroke practice. The fittest player can fall an easy prey to an opponent of inferior physique but far superior strokes. Take any Oxford and Cambridge boat race for an example. Which is the crew we find lying exhausted over their stretchers at the finish? The losing crew. But that doesn't mean for one moment that they were any less fit than the other crew. They had rowed themselves out trying to compete with a crew of superior skill and rowing ability. So, quite apart from attaining the highest degree of physical fitness possible, it is still more important that a potential champion shall perfect his or her strokes to the highest degree possible. In both of these desiderata British players since the Second World War have been far behind their American and Australian opponents. The will to win has been there, but there has not been the same willingness to undergo the drudgery, the "road work" so to speak, which lies behind the success of a champion boxer or a champion tennis player. "Il faut souffrir pour être belle!"

I can't think how many matches I have watched since World War II between American women and British women where, with the score standing at four-all, or set-all, a crisis is reached—and decided invariably against us either through lack of physical condition or disloyalty of stroke production.

Miss Betty Nuthall, the only Englishwoman ever to win the singles championship of the United States, learnt these lessons the hard way. At the age of sixteen she had beaten Mrs. Mallory, the famous American champion, at Wimbledon. She played for Britain at Forest Hills in the Wightman Cup of 1927 and much distinguished herself by beating Miss Helen Jacobs in the third single. In the next year's match at

Wimbledon Miss Jacobs very easily reversed the result. In 1929 Miss Nuthall played the second single for Britain in the Wightman Cup at Forest Hills and played splendidly against both Helen Wills and Helen Jacobs without getting a set from either. In 1930 Miss Nuthall went over to America on her own to have another crack at the American championships. She skipped and practised hard and had never been fitter or more in tune with her strokes than when she won both the singles and doubles championships of the United States that year.

After the Second World War Britain's women players lacked something of that determined will to win—which showed itself particularly in their doubles game, which was lacking in aggression and team-work.

There are, of course, two distinct types of amateur lawn tennis. There is the type which has, as its objective, a world championship. That type of tennis demands an early start, in most cases beginning with a course of instruction from a qualified coach, great application, strenuous training and varied competition. It is that type of tennis about which this book is most concerned, because it is around the champions that the history of the game has been built. It is a game of youth and high endeavour. But there is quite a different form of lawn tennis which flourishes in the clubs, the schools and the public parks, and which can be played and enjoyed almost literally from the cradle to the grave. It is a recreational amusement played not too seriously but with just sufficient competitive interest to make it attractive.

On the courts of the All-England Club at Wimbledon, when the captains and the kings have departed, and the members are free really to enjoy themselves, one can often see a doubles match in progress on some outside court, where four players, shorter in wind though in memory long, whose combined ages may be far exceeding the double century mark, are perhaps fighting out some ancient feud that once thrilled the Centre Court and even now may make some passing spectator stop and cheer. The great beauty of the game of lawn tennis is that, like cricket, it's a game for everyone. Rugby football is a grand game for boys and young men, but after thirty the ground becomes too hard and bones become too brittle—

and the over-thirties perforce have to become spectators. But lawn tennis can be played and enjoyed by boys and girls, men and women, tigers or rabbits, of all degrees of excellence and of all ages.

And the fact that British lawn tennis has a centre in Wimbledon, to which the whole world flocks every year as a matter of course, gives the British game a great focus and a great tradition which is recognised and admired by every lawn tennis enthusiast from abroad who has ever visited these shores. The fact that the Royal Family have taken such a close interest in Wimbledon still further enhances its reputation as a great national institution. So—Carry on Wimbledon! and Carry on Lawn Tennis!

INDEX

The numerals in **heavy type** *refer to the* **figure numbers** *of the illustrations*

~ 236 ~

~ 238 ~